With Fire and Sword

W. T. Sherman

With Fire and Sword

The American Civil War Experiences of a Soldier
of the 5th Iowa Infantry

S. H. M. Byers

LEONAUR

With Fire and Sword
The American Civil War Experiences of a Soldier of the 5th Iowa Infantry
by S. H. M. Byers

First published under the title
With Fire and Sword

Leonaur is an imprint of Oakpast Ltd
Copyright in this form © 2012 Oakpast Ltd

ISBN: 978-1-78282-014-7 (hardcover)
ISBN: 978-1-78282-015-4 (softcover)

http://www.leonaur.com

Publisher's Notes

Contents

Preface

In war some persons seek adventures; others have them in spite of themselves. It happened that the writer of this book belonged to a regiment that seemed to be always in the midst of great experiences. It was, in fact, one of the few regiments that absolutely fought themselves out of existence. It was mustered in a thousand strong; it lost seven hundred and seventy-seven men by death, wounds, and disease. The fragment that was left over was transferred to a cavalry command. When the writer finally escaped from prison, after many months of confinement and many thrilling adventures both in prison and in the army of the enemy, he was mustered out as a "supernumerary officer." His command had ceased to exist. He was literally the *last man of the regiment*. Of the eighty of his regiment who had been taken to prison with him all but sixteen were dead. Of the nine captured from his own company all were dead but one.

While with his command he had served as a private soldier, as sergeant, and as adjutant. On escaping from prison he was for a time on General Sherman's staff and was selected to run down the Cape Fear River and carry the great news of Sherman's successes to the people of the North.

He kept a diary every day in the four years of war and adventure. The substance of the facts related here is from its pages; occasionally they are copied just as they are there set down. The book is not a history of great army movements, it is simply a true tale of the thrilling experiences of a subordinate soldier in the midst of great events.

S. H. M. Byers.

CHAPTER 1

My Enlistment in the Union Army

I am writing down these sketches of adventures of mine from a daily journal or diary kept by me throughout the four years of the Civil War. Its pages are crumpled and old and yellow, but I can read them still.

Fate so arranged it that I was the very first one to enlist in my regiment, and it all came about through a confusion of names. A patriotic mass-meeting was held in the court-house of the village where I lived. Everybody was there, and everybody was excited, for the war tocsin was sounding all over the country. A new regiment had been ordered by the governor, and no town was so quick in responding to the call as the village of Newton. We would be the very first. Drums were beating at the mass-meeting, fifes screaming, people shouting. There was a little pause in the patriotic noise, and then someone called out, "Myers to the platform!" "Myers! Myers! Myers!" echoed a hundred other voices. Mr. Myers never stirred, as he was no public speaker. I sat beside him near the aisle. Again the voices shouted "Myers! Myers!" Myers turned to me, laughed, and said, "They are calling you, Byers," and fairly pushed me out into the aisle. A handful of the audience seeing Myers would not respond, did then call my own name, and both names were cried together. Some of the audience becoming confused called loudly for me. "Go on," said Myers, half-rising and pushing me toward the platform.

I was young,—just twenty-two,—ambitious, had just been admitted to the bar, and now was all on fire with the newly awakened patriotism. I went up to the platform and stood by the big drum. The American flag, the flag that had been fired on by the South, was hanging above my head. In a few minutes I was full of the mental champagne that comes from a cheering multitude. I was burning with excitement, with patriotism, enthusiasm, pride, and my enthusiasm lent power to the words I uttered. I don't know why nor how, but I was moving my audience. The war was not begun to put down slavery, but what in the beginning had been an incident I felt in the end would become a cause.

The year before I had been for many months on a plantation in Mississippi, and there with my own eyes had seen the horrors of slavery. I had seen human beings flogged; men and women bleeding from an overseer's lash. Now in my excitement I pictured it all. I recalled everything. "And the war, they tell us," I cried, "is to perpetuate this curse!" In ten minutes after my stormy words one hundred youths and men, myself the first, had stepped up to the paper lying on the big drum and had put down our names for the war.

We all mustered on the village green. Alas, not half of them were ever to see that village green again! No foreboding came to me, the enthusiastic youth about to be a soldier, of the "dangers by flood and field," the adventures, the thrilling scenes, the battles, the prisons, the escapes, that were awaiting me.

Now we were all enthusiasm to be taken quickly to the front, to the "seat of war." We could bide no delay. Once our men were on the very point of mobbing and "egging" our great, good Governor Kirkwood, because for a moment he thought he would be compelled to place us in a later regiment. However, we were immediately started in wagons for the nearest railroad, fifty miles away.

At the town of Burlington, on the 15th of July, 1861, we were mustered into the service as Company B of the Fifth Iowa Infantry. Our colonel, W. H. Worthington, was a military martinet from some soldier school in Kentucky. His sympathies were with his native South. Why he was leading a Northern regiment was a constant mystery to his men.

The regiment spent scant time in Burlington, for in a little while we were whisked down the Mississippi River in a steamer to St. Louis, and soon joined the army of Frémont, organizing at Jefferson City to march against General Price, who was flying toward Springfield with the booty he had gained in his capture of Mulligan and his men at Boonville. Now all began to look like war. Missouri was neither North nor South; she was simply hell, for her people were cutting one another's throats, and neighbouring farmers killed each other and burned each other's homes. The loyal feared to shut their eyes in sleep; the disloyal did not know if a roof would be above their heads in the morning. Brothers of the same family were in opposing armies, and the State was overrun by Southern guerrillas and murderers. The Quantrells, the James Brothers, and other irregular and roaming bands of villains rode everywhere, waylaying, bushwhacking, and murdering.

We followed General Price's army to the Ozark Mountains, marching day and night—the nights made hideous by the burning of homes on the track of both the armies, while unburied corpses lay at the roadside. We marched half the nights and all the days and just as we got close enough to fight, the Washington politicians caused Frémont to be removed from his command. Frémont had been ahead of his time. He had freed some slaves, and the dough-faced politicians were not yet ready for action of that character.

The campaign had been to no purpose. Some of our regiment, indignant at the removal of their general, had to be guarded to prevent mutiny and disorder. Now we turned about and made the long march back to the Missouri River. Half that cold winter was spent near Syracuse, in guarding the Pacific Railway. We lived in wedge tents, and spite of the cold and snow and storm, our squads by turn tramped for miles up and down the railroad in the darkness every night. What terrible tales, too, we had in our little tents that winter, of the deeds of Quantrell's men. It did not seem possible that the South could set loose a lot of murderers to hang on the skirts of our army, to "bushwhack" an honourable foe, burn villages, destroy farms, and drive whole counties into conditions as frightful as war was in the Middle Ages. Only savage Indians fought that way. Yet Quantrell's band of murderers was said to be on the payroll of the Confederate States. Here and there, however, his guerrilla outlaws met with awful punishment, and horrible incidents became the order of the day and night.

I recall now how a prize was once offered by one of our commanders for the head of a certain man among those desperate murderers, a *desperado* with a band of men that knew no mercy. His troop of riders had ambuscaded almost scores of our soldiers, and innocent farmers who did not happen to like his ways were strung up to trees as unceremoniously as one would drown a kitten. The offered prize of a thousand dollars stimulated certain of our men in taking chances with this beast of the Confederacy, and a corporal of our cavalry learned of the *desperado's* occasional visits at night to his home, only a dozen miles away from where we were camped. Several nights he secretly watched from a thicket near the cabin for the bandit's return. Once in the darkness he heard a horse's hoofs, and then a man dismounted and entered at the door. The evening was chilly, and a bright fire in the open fireplace of the cabin shone out as the man entered.

The corporal, who had disguised himself in an old gray overcoat, knocked for entrance, and pretended to be a sick Confederate going on a furlough to his home not far away. He was cautiously admitted and given a seat by the open fire. He had no arms, and to the bandit and his wife his story of sickness and a furlough seemed probable enough. The two men and the one woman sat in front of the fireplace talking for an hour. The corporal, with the guerrilla sitting within a few feet of him, thought of the prize, and of his comrades murdered by this man. But what could he do? Suddenly the thought came, "I must kill or be killed." Outside there was only darkness and silence; inside the cabin, the low voices of these three people and the flickering fire.

The corporal glanced about him. There was no gun to be seen that he could seize. The guerrilla's big revolver hung at his belt. While sitting thus, a bit of burning wood rolled out onto the hearth. The guerrilla stooped over to put it in its place. Instantly the corporal saw his chance and, springing for the iron poker at the fireside, dealt the guerrilla a blow on the head that stretched him dead on the cabin floor. In an instant his big jack-knife was out of his pocket and in the presence of the screaming wife the brute severed the man's head from his body. Then he left the cabin, mounted his horse in the thicket, and in the darkness carried his ghostly trophy into camp. It is a horrible ride to think of, that dozen miles, with the bleeding head of a murdered man on the saddle bow.

So the awful things went on all that winter in Missouri. As for myself, I was tramping about as a corporal, helping in a small way to keep the great railroad free from marauders and in possession of the Union army.

I don't know how it happened, but one morning our colonel, who had always treated me with extreme gruffness, though he well knew I did my duties with patriotic zeal, sent for me to come to his tent. I was a little alarmed, not knowing what was about to happen to me. The colonel called me by name as I entered, saluting him cap in hand, and for once he actually smiled.

"Corporal," he said dryly, as if suddenly regretting his smile, "I have noticed that you always did the duty assigned you with promptness. I need a quartermaster sergeant. You are the man."

I was almost paralyzed with astonishment and pleasure. I stood stock still, without a word of gratitude. At last, recovering myself, I explained that I had enlisted expecting to fight, and not to fill some easy position with the trains.

"If I could only be allowed to find a substitute," I ventured to say, "in case of a fight, so I might share the danger with my comrades, I would like the promotion."

Again the colonel tried to smile. "You probably will change your mind; you will find excitement enough," he remarked, dismissing me.

I was hardly installed in my new post when to my surprise I was ordered by the colonel to take a good horse and ride twelve miles across the lone prairies and carry a message to a command at the village of Tipton. Instantly my mind was excited with the hopes of an adventure. I don't know, even now, just why I was selected for the venturesome undertaking. I knew there was scarcely a road and not a house in the whole distance. I knew, too, the whole country was full of murderous guerrillas. But nevertheless I was full of elation. This was the kind of a thing I had hoped for when I enlisted.

Light flakes of snow were falling when, with exultant spirits, I started from the camp. The trip outward proved uneventful, for nothing happened to me on my way. As I was returning, however, at a point halfway across the prairie I was surprised to see a man in gray, probably a guerrilla, ride out of a long slough or hollow to my left and gallop into the road directly ahead of me. He was in complete gray uniform, wore a sabre, and had revolvers at his saddle bow. The man glanced back at me, and I saw him reaching for his pistols. "Here comes my first fight in the war," I thought instantly, "out here alone on the prairie." Save my one half-loaded revolver, strapped to my waist, I was unarmed. The stranger, without firing, galloped faster. I, too, galloped faster, the distance between us remaining about the same. Each of us now had a pistol in his hand, but it looked as if each were afraid to commence the duel.

If the stranger checked his horse to give him breath, I checked mine. If he galloped again, I, too, put spurs to my animal. Imagining that other guerrillas must be lurking quite near, I was not over-anxious to bring on the engagement, and I suppose the armed man felt much the same way, for he could not have thought that I was in such a place absolutely alone. So neither fired. We just looked at each other and galloped. Finally we approached a little wood, and in a twinkling he turned into a path and was out of sight. I did not care to follow him to his hiding-place just then, and quickly galloped to our camp a few miles off.

Before midnight that night I, with a dozen of my regiment, surrounded the little wood and a cabin secreted in its centre. Approaching, we looked into the windows, and, sure enough, there, roasting his feet in front of an open fire, sat my rider of the day. When three of us suddenly entered the house and demanded his surrender he sprang for a rifle that stood like a poker by the fireside, aimed it at me, and shouted "Never! Surrender yourself." A bayonet that instant against his breast brought him to terms, however. There followed a little farewell scene between him and his wife, who poured bottles of wrath on the heads of the "bluecoats," and our captive—my captive—was hurried to the guardhouse at the camp. It had been a perfectly bloodless encounter, but next morning it turned out that I had by chance captured one of the most dangerous guerrillas in Missouri.

CHAPTER 2

We leave Missouri and Go South

It was a trifling incident, this capture, compared with the dreadful things I have referred to as going on in Missouri that memorable first year of the Civil War. A great volume would not contain the record of them all. The first dead men I saw while in the army were eight Missouri farmers murdered by guerrillas and left lying in the hot sun and dust at the roadside. The sight moved me as no great battle ever did afterward.

One half of the male population of Missouri was trying to kill the other half. They were not opponents from different far-off sections fighting, but near neighbours, and nothing seemed too awful or too cruel for them to do. How I pitied the women and children who lived in the State in those awful days!

General Sherman's designation of war as "hell" found more confirmation in the dreadful raids, outrages, and murders by Quantrell's guerrillas in Missouri than in the bloodiest battles of the four years' conflict.

Now for months my regiment, with others, had chased up and down, and all over that unhappy old State of Missouri, trying to capture and punish these bands of murderers. On the old steamboat *War Eagle*, too, we paddled for weeks along the "Muddy Missouri" River, landing every here and there to have a little brush with guerrillas who had fired on our boat from the banks or from secret recesses in the woods. It was rare that we could catch them or have a real fight. Their kind of war meant ambuscades and murder.

At last an end came to this dreadful guerrilla-chasing business in Missouri so far as we were concerned, anyway. We were to stop running after Price's ubiquitous army too. We were no longer to be the victims of ambuscades and night riding murderers.

The glad news came to my regiment that we were to be transferred to the South, where the real war was.

One morning we left the cold and snow, where we had lived and shivered in thin tents all the winter, left the thankless duty of patrolling railroads in the storm at midnight, and marched in the direction of St. Louis. A long, cold, miserable march it was too, hurrying in the daytime and freezing in our bivouacs in the snow and woods at night. Many a man we left to sicken and die at some farmhouse by the roadside. Our destination was New Madrid, where we were to be a part of Pope's army in the siege and capture of that town.

As we were about to embark on boats at St. Louis we beheld in the snow and storm many steamers anchored out in the pitiless waters of the Mississippi River. These vessels were loaded with shivering thousands in gray and brown uniforms, the prisoners whom General Grant had captured at the battle of Fort Donelson. There were twelve or fifteen thousand of them. Seeing this host of prisoners made us feel that at last the Union army had a general, although we had scarcely heard of U. S. Grant before. This army of prisoners taken in battle was his introduction to the world.

Shortly we were before New Madrid, and the siege conducted by General Pope commenced. The town was defended by strong forts and many cannon, but its speedy capture by us helped to open up the Mississippi River. It was a new experience to us, to have cannonballs come rolling right into our camp occasionally. Yet few men were injured by them. We were in more danger when a fool officer one day took our brigade of infantry down through a cornfield to assault a gunboat that lay in a creek close by.

The Rebel commander had expected us, and had his grape shot and his hot water hose, and such things all ready for us. We went out of that cornfield faster than we went in. This was real war, the thing my regiment had been so longing for, in place of chasing murderers and guerrillas in Missouri.

We entered New Madrid one morning before daylight. The enemy had left in awful haste. I recall finding a dead Rebel officer, lying on a table in his tent, in full uniform. He had been killed by one of our shells. A candle burned beside him, and his cold hands closed on a pencil note that said, "Kindly bury this unfortunate officer." His breakfast waited on a table in the tent, showing how unexpected was his taking off.

Our victory was a great one for the nation, and it put two stars on the shoulder straps of General Pope. It made him, too, commander of the Eastern army.

A comrade in Company A of my regiment had been wounded a few days before and had died in the enemy's hands. I now found his grave. At its head stood a board with this curious inscription: "This man says he was a private in the Fifth Iowa Regiment. He was killed while trying to attend to other people's business."

Our command was now hurried to the Shiloh battlefield, of course too late to be of any use. But we took part in the long, wonderful, and ridiculous siege of Corinth, under Halleck, when our great army was held back by red tape, martinets, and the fear of a lot of wooden guns that sat on top of the enemy's breastworks, while that enemy, with all his men, and with all his guns, and bag and baggage, was escaping to the south. Our deeds were no credit to anybody, though here and there we had a little fight.

One incident of great importance, however, happened to my regiment here. It was the death of our colonel. One night when he was going the rounds of the picket lines out in the woods he was shot dead by one of our own men. The sentinel who did the killing declared that Rebels had been slipping up to his post all night, and when he would hail with "Who goes there?" they would fire at him and run into the darkness. He resolved to stand behind a tree the next time and fire without hailing. By some accident Colonel Worthington and his adjutant were approaching this sentinel from the direction of the enemy. Suddenly the sentinel held his gun around the tree and fired. The bullet struck the colonel in the forehead, killing him instantly. As he fell from his horse the adjutant sprang to the ground and cried, "Who shot the officer of the day?"

"I fired," exclaimed the sentinel, and he then told of his experiences of the night. He was arrested, tried, and acquitted. Yet there were many among us who believed that the colonel had been intentionally murdered. He was one of the most competent colonels in the army, but among his soldiers he was fearfully unpopular. He was, however, a splendid disciplinarian, but this was something the volunteers did not want. In their minds the colonel had been only a petty tyrant, and not even wholly loyal. With a different disposition he certainly would have been a distinguished soldier. He was one of the most military-looking men in the whole army, but friends he had none. More than once his life had been threatened by soldiers who regarded themselves as having been treated badly by him.

17

His body was brought into camp the next morning and lay in his tent in state. He was given a military funeral, and the horse that was bearing him when he was killed was led behind his coffin.

After his death numbers of the men of the regiment were indignant, when they found among his papers warrants and commissions intended by the governor for them, commissions that had never been delivered. Their promotions had never come about. Now they knew why.

Worthington was succeeded by Colonel C. L. Matthies, one of the bravest, best, and most loved commanders of our army. Later Matthies was made a general, and at the close of the war died of wounds received in battle.

Although I was quartermaster sergeant of the regiment, I was always careful that this should not keep me away from the command when enduring hard marches or when engagements were coming on. When in camp I kept my rifle in one of the ammunition wagons (of several of which I had charge), but if the alarm sounded my rifle was on my shoulder and I was the private soldier in the ranks of the company. I deserved no special credit for this. I was only doing my duty. We had muzzle-loading Whitney rifles and bayonets. The equipment and rations we carried in weight would have been a respectable load for a mule.

CHAPTER 3

The Battle of Iuka

All that summer, after taking Corinth, we chased up and down the State of Mississippi, trying to get fair battle with the Rebel army. At last the chance came, and for my regiment it was an awful one—the battle of Iuka.

The Battle of Iuka took place on the 19th of September, 1862. It was fought by a handful of the troops of General Rosecrans against half the army of General Price. Grant was only a few miles away, but although commander-in-chief, he knew nothing of the hardest-fought battle of the Civil War until it was over.

One morning before daylight while camped in the woods near Jacinto half expecting to be attacked, we heard that Price's army was in Iuka, some eighteen miles away, and that if we would hurry there and attack from one side, General Grant, with Ord's troops, would attack from another side. How eagerly the regiment made the forward march on that beautiful autumn day! The woods were in their fairest foliage, and it seemed too lovely a day for war and bloodshed. The bugles played occasionally as the men hurried along, but not a shot was fired. No noise like war fell on the soldiers' ears as they tramped over the beautiful country road toward the Tennessee River. They had time for reflection as they marched, and they knew now they were going to battle. There had been no time for letters or farewells, and each thought the other one, not himself, most likely to fall in the coming engagement.

There were only 482 of my little regiment now marching there, hoping, almost praying, the enemy might only wait. How little anyone dreamed that before the sun set 217 of that little command would be stretched dead or dying among the autumn leaves!

It was just two o'clock when the regiment ran on to the army of

19

the enemy, lying in line right across the road close to Iuka. My own regiment was in the advance. Instantly it, too, was in line of battle across that road, and in a few minutes absolutely the fiercest little conflict of the war began. Our brigade was fearfully outnumbered. Rosecrans, had ten thousand soldiers within five miles of the battlefield, yet let three or four small regiments and a battery do all the fighting. Ten miles away, in another direction, lay General Grant and General Ord, with many other thousands, as silent as if paralyzed. An unlucky wind blew, they said, and the sound of our cannon, that was to have been the signal for them to attack also, was unheard by them.

Charge after charge was made upon our little line, and the Eleventh Ohio Battery, which the regiment was protecting, was taken and retaken three times. There were no breastworks, yet that one little brigade of Hamilton's division stood there in the open and repulsed assault after assault. It was the Iowa, the Missouri, and the Ohio boys against the boys of Alabama and Mississippi, and the grass and leaves were covered with the bodies in blue and gray. Not Balaklava, nor the Alma, saw such fighting. It was a duel to the death. For hours the blue and the gray stood within forty yards of each other and poured in sheets of musketry. Every horse of the battery at the left of my regiment was killed, and every gunner but one or two was shot and lying among the debris. No battery in the whole four years' war lost so many men in so short a time. Antietam, Gettysburg, the Wilderness, could show nothing like it. Only the setting sun put an end to what was part of the time a hand to hand conflict. One daring Rebel was shot down and bayoneted clear behind the line of Company B, where he had broken through to seize the flag of my regiment.

That night the enemy slipped away, leaving hundreds and hundreds of his dead and wounded on the field. With a few lanterns our men then went about and tried to gather up the wounded; the dead were left till morning. There were 782 Union men lying there in their blood that long night, 608 of them out of a single small brigade. While mothers and sisters at home were praying for the safety of these dear ones at the front, their spirits that night were leaving their torn bodies in the dark and ascending heavenward. Five of my eight messmates of the day before were shot. It was not a question who was dead, or wounded, but who was *not*. Fifteen officers of our little half regiment were dead or wounded. The enemy lost more than one thousand men in trying to destroy that single brigade and its Ohio battery.

The burying party the next morning found nineteen dead Rebels lying together at one place. At another spot 182 Rebel corpses lay in a row covered by tarpaulins. The enemy had not had time to bury them.

It was a principle among our generals that if a command fought well in a battle or got cut all to pieces, that was the particular command to be put at the very front in the next hard scrap. And so it was that within two weeks my regiment was placed outside the breastworks at Corinth, to wait and receive another awful assault.

The night before the battle of Corinth the Fifth Iowa Regiment lay across the Purdy road, in the bright moonlight. I remained awake all night, talking with a comrade who shared my blanket with me. Poor Jimmy King! he survived the war only to be murdered later on a plantation in Mississippi. As we lay there in the wagon road, the awful losses of my regiment at Iuka kept us thinking there in the moonlight what would happen on the morrow. When morning came the firing opened, and for all that day the battle raged fiercely at the left and center left, we getting the worst of it, too. The Rebels were charging works that they themselves had built when they held the town during Halleck's siege. General Haccelman and many other of our officers had fallen. Our own division, though fighting some, had lost but few men.

That evening an order came for us—Hamilton's Division—to assault the enemy's left flank at midnight. Before the hour came, however, the move was decided to be too dangerous, and we changed our position to one nearer the forts. All the night we lay there under the brightest moonlight I ever saw. Under the same quiet moonlight, and only six hundred yards away from us, also lay the victorious Rebel army. They believed Corinth as good as taken, but they had only captured our outer lines of forts. Yet it looked very bad for us. Every house in town was full of our wounded and our dead lay everywhere.

Once in the night I slipped away from the bivouac and hurried to the old Tishimingo Hotel, to see a lieutenant of my company, who had been shot through the breast. Never will I forget the horrible scenes of that night. The town seemed full of the groans of dying men. In one large room of the Tishimingo House surgeons worked all the night, cutting off arms and legs. I could not help my friend. It was too late, for he was dying. "Go back to the regiment," he said, smiling, "all will be needed."

It was a relief to me to get back into the moonlight and out of the horror, yet out there lay thousands of others in line, only waiting the daylight to be also mangled and torn like these. The moon shone so brightly the men in the lines, tired though they were, could scarcely sleep. There the thousands lay, the blue and the gray, under the same peaceful moon, worshiping the same God, and each praying for dear ones North and South they would never again see. God could not answer the prayers of the men in both armies that night. Had He done so, all would have been killed on the morrow. At early daybreak I again went to see my lieutenant. As I entered the building a cannonball from the enemy crashed through the house and killed four soldiers by the stairway. My friend, with many others, was being carried out to die elsewhere.

It was soon full day. In one of the rooms I saw the floors, tables, and chairs covered with amputated limbs, some white and some broken and bleeding. There were simply bushels of them, and the floor was running blood. It was a strange, horrible sight,—but it was war. Yes, it was "hell." I hastened back to the lines. Nine o'clock came, and now we knew that the great assault was to be made. We looked for it against our own division, as we lay in the grass waiting. Suddenly we heard something, almost like a distant whirlwind. My regiment rose to its feet, fired a few moments at scattering Rebels in our front, and were amazed to see a great black column, ten thousand strong, moving like a mighty storm-cloud out of the woods and attacking the forts and troops at our left. Instantly we changed direction a little and, without further firing, witnessed one of the greatest assaults of any war. It was the storming of Fort Robinett.

The cloud of Rebels we had seen divided itself into three columns. These recklessly advanced on the forts, climbing over the fallen trees and bending their heads against the awful storm of grape and canister from all our cannon. A perfect blaze of close range musketry, too, mowed them down like grass. Even a foe could feel pity to see brave men so cruelly slaughtered.

When the assault had failed and the noise of battle was stilled, I hurried down in front of Robinett. My canteen was full of water and I pressed it to the lips of many a dying enemy—enemy no longer. Our grape shot had torn whole companies of men to pieces. They lay in heaps of dozens, even close up to the works. General Rogers, who had led a brigade into the hopeless pit, lay on his back, dead, with his flag in his hand. *He was the fifth one to die carrying that flag.* When I reached him some cruel one had stripped him of his boots. Another had taken his fine gold watch.

In this attack on Corinth the brave Southerners lost 5000 wounded, and we buried 1423 of their dead on the battlefield. Our own loss
had been 2200 dead and wounded. That night I stood guard under
an oak tree on the battlefield among the unburied dead. Many of the
wounded, even, had not yet been gathered up. The moon shone as
brightly as the night before, while thousands who had lain there under
its peaceful rays before the battle were now again sleeping, but never
to waken.

Our regiment now pursued the flying Rebels with great vigour.
The quantities of broken batteries, wagons, tents, knapsacks, guns, etc.,
strewn along the roads behind them were immense. At the Hatchie
River the Rebels were momentarily headed off by a division under
Hurlbut that had hurried across from Bolivar. A seven hours' battle
was fought at the bridge, but the Rebels got away in another direction. Possibly the best friend I had in the world, save my kin, was killed
at that bridge. It was Lieutenant William Dodd, a classmate in school.
His head was shot off by a cannonball just as his regiment was charging at the bridge.

The pursuit of the enemy was being pushed with vigour when
the army was ordered to desist and return to camp. It was an astound-
ing order, as it was in our power to destroy the defeated and flying
columns. That order was one of the mistakes of Grant's earlier days as
a commander. Indeed, we of the rank and file had little confidence
in Grant in those days. We reflected that at Shiloh he was miles away
from the battlefield at the critical moment. Sherman had saved the
Union army from destruction there. At Iuka, Grant, though commander, did not even know a battle was going on. At Corinth he was
miles away, and now, when we had the enemy almost within our grasp,
he suddenly called us back. Rosecrans protested. It was in vain. The
order, more imperative than before, was repeated. It required months,
and great events, to make Grant the hero of the army which he afterward became.

This entry I find in my diary in one of those days:

> Our commander of the district is General U. S. Grant, who
> took Donelson; but aside from that one hour's fighting, and a
> little fighting at Shiloh, the troops know little about him. Rose-
> crans is at present the hero of this army, and, with him leading
> it, the boys would storm Hades.

With the mercury at one hundred, the dust in the roads ankle deep, and the whole atmosphere yellow and full of it, the regiments exhausted by the pursuit, and yet disgusted at our recall, slowly tramped their way back to Corinth. Now I visited my wounded companions in the hospital. On inquiry for certain ones I learned that they were dead and lying out in the improvised graveyard nearby.

For some reason the dead at Hatchie Bridge were not buried. A week after the battle my brother rode by there on a cavalry expedition and made the horrible discovery that hogs were eating up the bodies of our dead heroes. *That too was war.*

We now camped on the edge of the town and went on building still other and greater forts. Many of the soldiers made huts for themselves. It was getting cooler now, and little fireplaces were built in the huts and tents. Brick was scarce, and in a few instances the men used the stone slabs from a graveyard close at hand. It seemed vandalism, but the dead did not need them and the living did.

CHAPTER 4

Holly Springs Burned Up

In a month's time, or by November 2, 1862, the army, reorganized, our division led by Quimby, and Grant in command of the whole force, started on that very first disastrous campaign for the rear of Vicksburg. Grant had some thirty thousand soldiers to march with him by way of Grand Junction and Holly Springs, and another thirty thousand men, under Sherman, he sent down the Mississippi River to attack Vicksburg from another direction. We marched in mud and wind and rain till nearly Christmas, the enemy constantly retreating before us. We made a tremendous supply station at Holly Springs and left it in charge of a garrison. There were supplies there for a hundred thousand men, besides a million dollars' worth of captured cotton.

Just as we were confident of overtaking and destroying the enemy, we were stunned by the tidings that a great column of Rebel cavalry had dashed in behind our army. With torches and firebrands they had burned Holly Springs to the ground, and had destroyed all the army stores. There was not a potato or cracker or a pound of bacon left. How I remember that dark night when Van Dorn's cavalry got behind us in the country lanes of Mississippi! I had been started back to a hospital in Holly Springs, for my eyes had been inflamed for days. Just as my little freight train reached the suburb of what had been the town, the rear guard of the enemy rode out at the other side. The morning that I arrived there was nothing there but smoke, and ashes, and ruins, and a smell of coal oil over all. A million dollars' worth of our army supplies had been burned up in a night. The pretty town, too, was in ashes, and Van Dorn's bold cavalry swung their sabres in the air and rode away laughing. General Grant's father and mother, in the town at the time on their way to visit their illustrious son with the advance of the army, were captured, but politely paroled and left among the ruins.

The loss of the town was a disgrace to the North. There was a fort there, solidly built of cotton bales and occupied by a colonel and a thousand troops. The colonel forgot what our ancestors did with cotton bales at New Orleans, and promptly threw up the sponge. But then Colonel Murphy was not General Jackson. With the loss of Holly Springs and the destruction of our base of supplies there was nothing for that whole army of Grant's to do but to trudge its weary way back to Corinth and Memphis, through the mud and the wind and the rain.

The tragical part of that campaign was taking place at the same moment down by the Yazoo River, right under the guns of Vicksburg. Grant, when he marched out of Memphis, had sent Sherman and thirty thousand men down the river in steamboats to attack Vicksburg from one side while he should hurry along with another thirty thousand men and pound it from the other side. Sherman and his heroes made the awful assaults at Chickasaw bayou we read of, never dreaming of the fiasco that had befallen the main army at Holly Springs. Not one word of the news ever reached him—and then in swamps and bayous his soldiers waded in water halfway to their necks and assaulted impregnable hills and breastworks. Two thousand men were killed or mangled to no purpose. Some of the heroic fighting of the war was done in that Yazoo slaughter pen, and then Sherman and his crippled army withdrew in utter failure.

Vicksburg was safe for awhile.

My own duty in that unlucky campaign with Grant had been to search the country in the neighbourhood of our camps and bivouacs for additional supplies. Many a time, with a dozen or twenty men for guards, and a couple of six-mule teams, we would venture miles from camp to confiscate bacon, flour, poultry, or whatever else a soldier could eat. On my return to the regiment with a wagon full of good things, the companies would set up a cheer for the quartermaster sergeant. The colonel always allowed me to choose the guards who should accompany me. Many a time our little squad got back to camp by the skin of their teeth, chased by guerrillas or some wandering band of Rebel cavalry. Our habit was, when we found a plantation with something to spare on it, to post sentinels in the lanes in every direction, while a few of us with the aid of the negroes loaded the wagons. If all went well, the procession, followed by the slaves we freed and took with us, went back to camp in state. Sometimes there was indecorous haste in getting home, owing to our sentinel firing his gun in warning of near danger. More than one of the boys of those venturous excursions, to this day, have not yet come back to camp.

On one of these excursions one day we were surprised by a little party of rangers, but we took their leader captive, and with him a fine Kentucky charger and a splendid rifle. The brigade colonel presented to me the rifle I myself had captured, for my "bravery," he said, but the splendid thoroughbred he took for himself. Alas! this rifle, the testimonial of my adventure, was burned up when the Rebel cavalry took Holly Springs. I had left it there to send North some day.

These excursions after food that I have described must have been the forerunners of Sherman's great forage parties later, on his "march to the sea." It was easy enough to feed an army that way, if men could be found to take the risk. Sherman's later forage parties were so strong that the risk was reduced to fun.

I copy from my diary here (1862):

Now the enemy is in front of us. He is on our flank and all around us. It is dangerous to venture a mile from camp alone. In fact, orders are strict for every man and every officer to stay close to his regiment day or night.

On all the plantations along our way in this campaign there are signs of war. The cotton gins, the fences, the barns, are all gone,—burned by raiders of both armies, who have scouted through this same country time and again. The weather is often gloomy; the fenceless fields are brown and naked; the big houses left standing on the plantations look lone and desolate. There is no song of birds. The army wagons, in long trains, and the soldiers in great strung-out columns of blue, go over the soft ground across the fields, along what once was lanes and country roads, almost in silence. Here and there a skirmish of musketry at some creek crossing or at some wood is the only noise heard. This state of Mississippi, like the whole South, sees the desolation of war. But the big, white, lone houses on the deserted lawns, with their low verandas about them, are not wholly unoccupied. Though the arms-bearing men of the country are every one in the army fighting us, the women and the children and the slaves are still at home. These slaves desert their mistresses and come into the Union camps at night by hundreds, bearing their bundles on their heads and their *pickaninnies* under their arms.

"As Rebel cavalry bands are rioting all around us, the strictest orders are given about leaving camp. But those who slipped away without leave the oftenest were themselves officers. Numbers of these went off almost nightly, to pay their devoirs to ladies whom they happened to admire at neighbouring plantations. These women, glad enough of the compliments of the Federal officers, let it be very clearly understood that they were nevertheless true-blue Rebels. Things as to the war were simply glossed over in conversation, and both the lady and the officer sometimes had a delightful evening, even if the delight on the officer's part was in violation of duty. Sometimes these visits led to ridiculous terminations. War is not all tragedy.

Again I copy from the journal of that December:

The other night three of the officers of our brigade, Captain H—— and Lieutenants D—— and O—— got themselves into a pretty mess by leaving camp to visit at a plantation. The laughable facts are these: We had stopped two or three days, to mend bridges over the Yocona River. General Grant had asked our brigade commander to report the names of three officers for promotion. Captain H—— and two lieutenants were selected. Among the private soldiers these men were not regarded as deserving honour. On the contrary, they were looked upon as common braggarts. Some politician at home, probably, had moved the wires for their promotion.

As it happened, these three officers were the worst offenders of all, as to leaving camp without orders for the purpose of visiting Rebel ladies at neighbouring plantations. Some of the staff heard of this and determined to unmask them. Some Rebel uniforms were secured from prisoners in our hands, and one dark night when the captain and his friends were away from camp at the home of a Mrs. S——, visiting, a dozen of us in disguise were sent to surround the house. Instantly there was a cry among the women of "guerrillas!" "Confederates!" "Confederates!" "Friends!" and a bonny blue Rebel flag was waved in the doorway.

We were indeed a desperate-looking lot, but the women met the supposed Rebel guerrillas almost with embraces. The captain and his two lieutenants we pulled from under the bed by their heels, and threatened them with instant death. The women begged us only not to kill them in the house. The officers, on their knees, pleaded for their lives. It was agreed that they should simply give up their swords, be paroled, and allowed to return to camp. At headquarters the next morning, in explanation of the loss of their swords, they told a wonderful and Falstaffian tale of being overwhelmed by Van Dorn's guerrillas the night before, and of their miraculous escape to camp. That moment they were confronted with their surrendered swords and their signatures to their paroles. There was a fine collapse at headquarters that morning. The names of the three gentlemen were sent to General Grant the same day, I understand. But not for promotion.

I had a little taste of life in the hospital that December. My eyes got worse. For a little time I was in a fine private home in Holly Springs, for the town, after its burning by Van Dorn, had been retaken by us. Every room in the house had its floors filled with the sick and the dying of both armies. Long years after that, while on shipboard returning from Europe, I made by chance the acquaintance of Mrs. Kate Sherwood Bonner, the authoress, who as a girl had lived in Holly Springs. We talked of the war times, and it transpired that the mansion where I had witnessed such distressful scenes among the dead and dying was her father's home.

I saw General Grant's father and mother there in Holly Springs daily. At the capture of the town they had been taken as stated, and released, the father on parole.

I was now sent to Memphis, as I was still in hospital. The hospital here was in the old Overton Hotel, which was crowded with hundreds of wounded. The room used as a dead house was filled every night. It was across the court and below my own room. I could see the corpses distinctly, as the window was left open. It was my habit, a strange one, when I awoke in the morning, to look over and count the corpses of men who had been carried in there while I had been sleeping. It seems now a ghastly business enough.

CHAPTER 5

The Laughable Campaign of the War

In a little time, February, 1863, Grant's army was again off to try for Vicksburg. This time it was to go on that campaign, so laughable now, but romantic always, called the "Yazoo Pass expedition." We were to go down the Mississippi River in big steamers to Helena, and there transfer ourselves on to a fleet of little steamers, cut the levee into the over-flooded country, and try floating a whole army a hundred miles across the plantations and swamps of Mississippi.

My eyes were well again, and I was happy to join our regiment and be one of the aquatic throng. Just as we were getting on to the boat at Memphis two of my company managed to get shot by the provost guard. They had been full of liquor, and refused to go to the steamer. They had been heroes at Iuka. How unlucky now to get crippled for life in a drunken brawl!

On the 22nd of March, near Helena, my regiment went aboard the pretty little schooner called the *Armada*. Shortly, dozens of these small boats, crowded with regiments, accompanied by gunboats, were floating about, awaiting the order to sail through a big cut that our engineers had made in the river levee and get down the pass into Moon Lake. The Mississippi was high and raging. All the low-lying country for half a hundred miles was flooded till it looked like a vast sea, with forests of trees standing in its midst. Here and there, too, a plantation, higher than the surrounding country, was noticeable. The first pass into Moon Lake was but a mile long. But through that pass swirled and roared the waters of the Mississippi, so suddenly let loose by the break in the levee.

At just four in the evening our little steamer got the order to turn out of the river and into the rushing waters of the pass. We would not have been more excited at being told to start over Niagara Falls. Our engines are working backward and we enter the crevasse slowly, but in five minutes the fearful, eddying current seized us, and our boat was whirled round and round like a toy skiff in a washtub. We all held our breath as the steamer was hurled among floating logs and against overhanging trees. In ten minutes the rushing torrent had carried us, backward, down into the little lake. Not a soul of the five hundred on board the boat in this crazy ride was lost. Once in the lake we stopped, and with amazement watched other boats, crowded with soldiers, also drift into the whirl and be swept down the pass. It was luck, not management, that half the little army was not drowned.

Now for days and days our little fleet coursed its way toward Vicksburg among the plantations, swamps, woods, bayous, cane-brakes, creeks, and rivers of that inland sea. Wherever the water seemed deepest that was our course, but almost every hour projecting stumps and trees had to be sawn off under the water to allow our craft to get through. Sometimes we advanced only four or five miles a day. At night the boat would be tied to some tall sycamore. Here and there we landed at some plantation that seemed like an island in the flood. The negroes on the plantation, amazed at our coming, wondered if it was the day of Jubilee or if it was another Noah's flood and that these iron gunboats arks of safety.

We soldiers, if not on duty pushing the boat away from trees, had nothing to do but sleep and eat and read. Most of the soldiers slept on the decks, on the guards, and on the cabin floors. Four of us had a little stateroom. I had with me a copy of Shakespeare, cribbed by one of the boys somewhere, and the Bard of Avon was never studied under stranger circumstances.

The Yazoo Pass, though not so crazy as the crevasse we had come through, was nevertheless bad and dangerous. Two of our craft sank to the bottom, but the soldiers were saved by getting into trees. All the boats were torn half to pieces. One day as we pushed our way along the crooked streams amid the vine-covered forests we ran onto a Rebel fort built on a bit of dry land. In front of it were great rafts that completely obstructed our way. An ocean steamer was also sunk in the channel in front of us. To our amazement we learned that it was the *Star of the West*, the ship that received the first shot fired in the war of the Rebellion. That was when it was trying to take supplies to Fort Sumter. Our gunboats shelled this "Fort Greenwood" in vain, and now Rebels were gathering around and behind us and guerrillas were beginning to fire on the boats. The waters, too, might soon subside, and our fleet and army be unable to get back into the Mississippi. We could not go ahead. Suddenly the orders came to turn about and steam as fast as possible to a place of safety.

By April 8 we had made the journey through the woods and cane-brake back to the pass. The picturesque farce was ended. We could now hunt some other road to Vicksburg. We know nothing of what the generals thought of this fiasco, but we private soldiers had great fun, and the long stay on the boats had been a rest from hard campaigning. We had not lost a man. A whole campaign and not a soldier lost!

CHAPTER 6

Grant's New Plan at Vicksburg

The attempt on Vicksburg was not to be given up. In the spring of 1863 the whole army moved down the Mississippi to begin one of the most noted campaigns of history.

A real sane notion had gotten hold of Grant, and of scarcely anyone else. That notion was, if possible, to get across the Mississippi *below* the town (Sherman had failed trying it above) and throw the whole army on to the fortifications at the rear. If the town's defenders should be bold and come out and fight us, so much the better. We wanted that.

Soon General Grant built long stretches of wagon roads and corduroy bridges that ran snakelike for forty miles among the black swamps, cane-brakes, and lagoons on the west bank of the Mississippi River. He then marched half his army down these roads to a point below Vicksburg, below Grand Gulf, and bivouacked them on the shore of the river. The other half, of which my regiment was a part, remained near the river above the city. Possibly we were twenty-five thousand men there.

One night these twenty-five thousand bivouacked along the levees of the great river were all in great excitement. "Coming events were casting their shadows before."

It must have been some great event was about to happen that April night of 1863, for the Assistant Secretary of War was there, and General Grant and General Sherman were there, waiting and watching in the greatest suspense. What was going to happen? Some one hundred and fifty private soldiers were going to perform a deed that should help make American history. The success of a whole army and the capture of the best fortified city on the American continent depended on the heroism of this handful of private soldiers on this April night.

No wonder the government at Washington sat by the telegraph and anxiously awaited every scrap of news sent from Grant's army before Vicksburg. He was to open the Mississippi River. That very day, almost, the government at Washington sent a letter urging General Grant to hurry. General Halleck telegraphed for the President:

"In my opinion *this is the most important operation of the war. To open the Mississippi River would be better than the capture of forty Richmonds.*"

General Grant realized the mighty things he had at stake.

But what availed it to collect his soldiers there? In front of him, in high flood, swept the mightiest river on the continent; he had not a boat to cross with, and the enemy laughed and dared him from the other side. His fleet of steamboats was forty miles and more up the river, and between him and that fleet were four miles of hostile batteries strong enough to blow a fleet to pieces. In fact, every hill, hollow, and secret place above and below the city hid a dozen cannon. All the way from Vicksburg down to Warrentown was a fort.

What could be done? Without some steamers on which to cross, the game was blocked, and Vicksburg, strong as Sebastopol itself, might stand there forever and the Mississippi River be blockaded to the end of the war. Two or three of Grant's ironclad gunboats had run past these awful batteries one night, their sides banged to pieces and their iron mail scooped up as if it had been made of putty. One of them was sunk. But these iron tubs could not serve as ferryboats for forty thousand men. Then, the scheme was proposed to cover some of the wooden steamboats with cotton bales and on a dark night try and rush them past the batteries. The boat captains, however, would not risk it with their own crews, even had they as a rule been willing, and so the commands of the army asked for *volunteers* from the private soldiers.

Desperate as the undertaking seemed, one hundred and fifty Union soldiers stepped forward and offered to run these steamboats past the guns. The writer was one of these volunteers. But too many had offered to take the risk. The required number was selected by lot, and the most I could do that historic night was to stand on the river levee in the dark and watch my comrades perform one of the most heroic acts of any war. It was hardly a secret. The whole army was excited over the desperate proposal. The enemy must have heard of it, and been doubly prepared to destroy us. "If Grant's attempt prove successful he can destroy the whole Confederate army, take Vicksburg, and open the Mississippi River." No wonder the Washington officials sat by the telegraph day and night just then awaiting great news.

The moon was down by ten o'clock of the night of April 16. Under the starlight one hardly saw the dark river or the cane-brakes, swamps, and lagoons along its border. The whole Northern fleet lay anchored in silence. Grant's army too, down below, was silent and waiting. A few miles below us lay Vicksburg, dark, sullen, and sleeping. Not a gun was being fired. A few lonesome Confederate river guards floated above the town in rowboats watching to give the alarm at the approach of any foe on the water.

Three mysterious looking Northern steamboats, with crews of volunteer soldiers on board, lay out in the middle of the Mississippi River in front of Milliken's Bend, a dozen miles above Vicksburg. Down in the dark hold of each vessel stand a dozen determined men. They have boards, and pressed cotton, and piles of gunny sacks beside them there, to stop up holes that shall be made pretty soon by the cannon of the enemy. They have none of war's noise and excitement to keep them up—only its suspense. They are helpless. If anything happens they will go to the bottom of the river without a word. Above the decks the pilot-houses are taken off and the pilot wheels are down by the bows, and the pilot will stand there wholly exposed. Lashed to the sides of each of the three little steamers are barges piled up with bales of hay and cotton. They look like floating breastworks. Anchored still a little further down the stream seven gunboats also wait in silence. They will lead these steamboats and try the batteries first. The boats must all move two hundred yards apart. That is the order.

All is suspense. For a little while the night grows darker and more silent; the moon now is down. The thousands of soldiers standing on the levee waiting, and watching to see them start, almost hold their breath. At the boats there is no noise save the gurgling of the water as it grinds past the hulls of the anchored vessels. That is all the noise the men waiting down in the dimly lighted hulls can hear. On a little tug, nearby, General Grant, the commander of the Western armies, waits and listens. The Assistant Secretary of War is at his side. In a yawl, farther down the stream, General Sherman ventures far out on the dark river to watch events. All is ready, all is suspense. Just then a lantern on the levee is moved slowly up and down. It is the signal to start. Down in Vicksburg the unexpectant enemy sleeps. Their guards out on the river, too, almost sleep; all is so safe. Quietly we lift anchors and float off with the current. Our wheels are not moving. There is a great bend in the river, and as we round it the river guard wakened, sends

35

up a rocket, other rockets too go up all along the eastern or Vicksburg shore. That instant, too, a gun is fired from a neighbouring bluff.
We are discovered. "Put on all steam," calls the captain, and our boats
move swiftly into the maelstrom of sulphur and iron, for the enemy
opens fire vigorously.

The enemy sets houses on fire all along the levee to illuminate the
river, bonfires are lighted everywhere, and suddenly the whole night
seems but one terrific roar of cannon. The burning houses make the
river almost as light as day. We see the people in the streets of the town
running and gesticulating as if all were mad; their men at the batteries
load and fire and yell as if every shot sunk a steamboat. On the west
side of the river the lagoons and cane-brakes look weird and dangerous. The sky above is black, lighted only by sparks from the burning
houses. Down on the river it is a sheet of flame. One of the steamers
and a few of the barges have caught fire and are burning up, the men
escaping in life-boats and by swimming to the western shore. The excitement of the moment is maddening, the heavy fire appalling, while
the musketry on the shore barks and bites at the unprotected pilots on
the boats. Ten-inch cannon and great columbiads hurl their shot and
shell into the cotton breastworks of the barges or through the rigging
of the steamers. The gunboats tremble from the impact of shot against
their sides, and at times the little steamers are caught in the powerful
eddies of the river and are whirled three times around right in front
of the hot firing batteries.

*Five hundred and twenty-five shells and cannonballs are hurled at the hur-
rying fleet.* The flash of the guns, the light of the blazing houses, make
the night seem a horrible tempest of lightning and thunder. Sherman,
sitting out there alone in his yawl on the dark river, has witnessed awful spectacles, but this is the sight of a lifetime. "It was," he exclaimed,
"*a picture of the terrible not often seen.*" And amid all this roar and thunder and lightning and crash of cannonballs above, the men down in
the holds of the boats—they are the real heroes—stand in the dim
candle-light waiting, helpless, ignorant of events, and in terrible suspense, while sounds like the crash of worlds go on above their heads.
Once some of them climb up to the hatchways and look out into the
night. One look is enough! What a sight! The whole Mississippi River
seems on fire, the roar of the gunboats answering the howling cannon
on the shore, the terrific lightnings from the batteries, the screeching
shells above the decks. It was as if hell itself were loose that night on
the Mississippi River. For one hour and thirty minutes the brave men

stood speechless in the holds of the boats while hell's hurricane went on above. They lived an age in that hour and a half, and yet a thousand of us in Grant's army tried to volunteer that we, too, might have this awful experience.

Daylight saw the little fleet safe below Vicksburg, where thousands of soldiers welcomed it with cheers. No such deed had ever been done in the world before. Only one boat and some barges were lost, and only a few of the soldiers were hurt. The cotton bales had proved a miracle of defense. In a week still other steamers, though with greater loss, passed the batteries.

We know the rest. On these same boats Grant's army would ferry across the Mississippi, and there on the other side fight five battles and win them all. Vicksburg will be surrounded and assaulted and pounded and its soldiers starved, till, on the nation's birthday, thirty thousand of its brave defenders will lay down their arms forever.

CHAPTER 7

Crossing the Mississippi on Gunboats and Steamers

Now that the boats were below the city, we were to begin the Vicksburg campaign in earnest. All the troops that had been left camped on the river levee above at Milliken's Bend hurried by roundabout roads through cane-brakes and swamps to the point where our little boats had anchored after running past the batteries that night. Here we joined the rest of the army, and the ferrying of thousands of soldiers across the great river day and night at once commenced.

My own regiment was put on to one of the iron gunboats and ferried over the Mississippi at a point close to Grand Gulf. Here our river navy had silenced the Rebel forts. It was the first gunboat I had ever seen. Its sides bore great scars, indentations made by the enemy's batteries on the preceding day. We hurried on and became a part of the reserve at the hot battle of Port Gibson, as we ourselves did no fighting. In a plantation yard, close by my regiment, lay our wounded as they were carried back from the front. It was a terrible sight. Many had been torn by shrapnel and lay there on the grass in great agony. Some seemed with their own hands to be trying to tear their mangled limbs from their bodies. The possession of all Vicksburg did not seem worth the pain and the agony I saw there that afternoon. That was war; and it was "hell," sure enough.

The next day, when the battle was over, I was at a negro cabin getting a loaf of corn bread. I suddenly heard a little cheering down by the river, where some men were putting down pontoons in place of the bridge burned by the enemy. I went down at once, and as I stood by the river bank I noticed an officer on horseback in full general's uniform. Suddenly he dismounted and came over to the very spot where I was standing. I did not know his face, but something told me it was Grant,—Ulysses Grant,—at that moment the hero of the Western army. Solid he stood, erect, about five feet eight in height, with square features, thin, closed lips, brown hair, brown beard, both cut short, and neat. "He must weigh one hundred and forty or fifty pounds. Looks just like the soldier he is. I think he is larger than Napoleon, but not much; he is not so dumpy, his legs are not so short, and his neck is not so short and thick. He looks like a man in earnest, and the Rebels think he is one."

This was the first time I saw Grant. I think I still possess some of the feeling that came over me at that moment as I stood so near to one who held our lives, and possibly his country's life, in his hands. How little I dreamed that someday I would have the great honour of sitting beside him at my own table. Yet this occurred.

Now he spoke, "Men, push right along; close up fast, and hurry over." Two or three men on mules attempted to wedge past the soldiers on the bridge. Grant noticed it, and quietly said, "Lieutenant, arrest those men and send them to the rear." Every soldier passing turned to gaze on him. But there was no further recognition. There was no McClellan begging the boys to allow him to light his cigar by theirs; no inquiring to what regiment that exceedingly fine marching company belonged; there was no Pope bullying the men for not marching faster, reproving officers for neglecting trivial details remembered only by martinets; there was no Bonaparte posturing for effect; no pointing to the pyramids, no calling the centuries to witness. There was no nonsense, no sentiment. Only a plain business man of the republic there for the one single purpose of getting that army across the river in the shortest time possible. In short, it was just plain General Grant, as he appeared on his way to Vicksburg.

On a horse nearby, and among the still mounted staff, sat the general's son, a bright-looking lad of perhaps eleven years. Fastened to his little waist by a broad yellow belt was his father's sword—that sword on whose clear steel was yet to be engraved "Vicksburg," "Spotsylvania," "The Wilderness," "Appomattox." The boy talked and jested with the bronzed soldiers near him, who laughingly inquired where we should camp that night; to which the young field marshal replied, "Oh, over the river."

"Over the river!" Ah, that night we slept with our guns in our hands, and another night, and another, saw more than one of our division, and of my own regiment, camped over the river—in that last tenting ground—where the *réveille* was heard no more forever.

My own command crossed the bridge that night by torchlight. It was a strange weird scene. Many of the Rebel dead—killed beyond the stream by our cannon before our approach—still lay at the roadside or in fields unburied. At one turn in the road my regiment marched close by a Rebel battery that had been completely destroyed. Men, horses, and all lay there dead in indiscriminate heaps.

The face of one boy lying there among the horses I shall never forget. It was daylight now, the bright sun was just rising, when I left the ranks a moment to step aside to see that boy. He was lying on his back. His face was young and fair, his beautiful brown hair curled almost in ringlets, and his eyes, brown and beautiful, were wide open; his hands were across his breast. A cannonball had in an instant cut away the top of his head in as straight a line as if it had been done with a surgeon's saw. There had been no time for agony or pain. The boy's lips were almost in a smile. It was a Mississippi battery that had been torn to pieces there, and it may be that in a home near by a mother stood that morning praying for her boy. The South had such war costs as well as the North.

My regiment now entered on all those rapid marches and battles in the rear of Vicksburg—Raymond, Jackson, Champion Hills, and the assaults on the breastworks about the city. For days we scarcely slept at all; it was hurry here and quickstep there, day or night. None of us soldiers or subordinates could tell the direction we were marching. We had few rations, little water, and almost no rest. We had left our base at the river, and in a large sense we were cut off and surrounded all the time. The capture of a Rebel scout at once changed everything. Through him Grant learned how hurrying divisions of the enemy were about to unite. A quick move could checkmate everything. Indeed, it was nothing but a great game of chess that was being played, only we, the moving pieces, had blood and life. At one time Grant's army was as likely to be captured as to capture. My regiment, like all the others, hurried along the country roads through dust that came to the shoe top.

The atmosphere was yellow with it. The moving of a column far away could be traced by it. We followed it in the way that Joshua's army followed the mighty cloud. As we passed farms where there was something to eat the captains would call out to a dozen men of the line to hurry in, carry off all they could, and pass it over to the companies still marching. It was a singular looking army. So whole regiments tramped along with sides of bacon or sheaves of oats on the points of their bayonets. We dared not halt. When we bivouacked, long after dark, often it was the dust of the roadside. We always lay upon our arms. Sometimes there was a little fire, oftener there was none. The fat bacon was eaten raw.

My regiment was in advance at the engagement at Raymond; also at Jackson. At Jackson it rained and thundered fearfully during the battle. A Rebel battery was on a green slope right in front of us, pouring a terrible shelling into us as we approached it from the Raymond road. The shocks of thunder so intermingled with the shocks from the guns that we could not tell the one from the other, and many times a sudden crash of thunder caused us all to drop to the ground, fearing a cannonball would cut its swath through the regiment. We were marching in columns of fours. Shortly, we formed line of battle, and in rushing to the left through a great cane-brake, while we were advancing in battle line under a fire of musketry, the order was given to lie down.

We obeyed quickly. How closely, too, we hugged the ground and the depression made by a little brook! While I lay there it happened that my major (Marshall) was close behind me on horseback. He had no orders to dismount. I could glance back and see his face as the bullets zipped over our heads or past him. He sat on his horse as quiet as a statue, save that with his right hand he constantly twisted his moustache. He looked straight into the cane-brake. He was a brave man. Could the enemy behind the forests of cane have seen where they were firing he would not have lived a minute. Shortly there was roaring of cannon and quick charges at the other side of the town. Jackson was won.

At daylight the next morning we hurried in the direction of Champion Hills. At our left, as we went down the road, the battlefield of the day before was strewn with corpses of our own men. In a few minutes the brave Seventeenth Regiment of Iowa had lost 80 men at this spot, out of 350 engaged in an assault. My friend Captain Walden received honourable mention, among others, for gallantry in this Jackson charge. A few hundred yards off I noticed a man in a field quite alone, digging in the ground. Out of curiosity I went to him and asked what he was doing alone when the regiments were all hurrying away. A brown blanket covered something nearby. He pointed to it and said that two of his brothers lay dead under that blanket. He was digging a grave for them. He went on with his work and I hurried to overtake my command. This was the 15th of May, 1863. I did not know it then, but shortly I was to see General Grant in the midst of battle. I was to see several other things, and feel some of them also.

My situation as to the Fifth Regiment was a peculiar one; being the quartermaster sergeant, I belonged to no company in particular. The good colonel, however, knowing my love for adventure, and that I was never lacking in duty, allowed me to attach myself to any company I liked, provided only, that there was a reliable substitute performing my duties with the train at the rear. I had no trouble in securing such a substitute, usually found among the slightly wounded soldiers.

Since we crossed the Mississippi I had marched and carried my rifle all the way,—had been in every skirmish and engagement. Sometimes I tramped along with my old Company B of Newton, sometimes I went with the extreme left of the regiment. I was no more heroic than all the others in the command, but I was fond of the risk and the excitement of battle. I would have resigned my warrant as quartermaster sergeant in a moment rather than miss a hard march or an engagement, let the chance be what it might. I think my love of adventure, and my seeking it so often away from my proper post of duty at the rear, was often the occasion of amused comment. Once when marching at the left I heard our surgeon, Carpenter, cry out to another officer riding beside him: "There's a fight today. Look out. The sign's sure. The quartermaster sergeant has got his gun."

None of us private soldiers now really knew in what direction we were marching. We heard only that the enemy was concentrating at Edwards Ferry Station, between us and Big Black River. General Crocker of my State was now leading our division, and the magnificent General McPherson commanded the army corps. The night of May 15 the division bivouacked in the woods by the side of a road that leads from Bolton toward Vicksburg. We marched hard and late that day. The morning of the 16th my regiment was up and getting breakfast long before daylight. The breakfast consisted of some wet dough cooked on the ends of ramrods; nothing more.

Troops were hurrying past our bivouac by daylight. Once I went out to the roadside to look about a bit. It was scarcely more than early daylight, yet cannon could occasionally be heard in the far distance, something like low thunder. As I stood there watching some batteries hurrying along I noticed a general and his staff gallop through the woods, parallel with the road. They were leaping logs, brush, or whatever came in their way. It was General Grant, hurrying to the front. Shortly came the orders, "Fall in!" and we too were hurrying along that road toward Champion Hills. By ten o'clock the sound of the cannon fell thundering on our ears, and we hurried all we could, as riders came back saying the battle had already begun. As we approached the field the sound of great salvos of musketry told us the hour had surely come. The sound was indeed terrible.

At the left of the road we passed a pond of dirty water. All who could broke ranks and filled canteens, knowing that in the heat of the fight we would need the water terribly. I not only filled my canteen, I filled my stomach with the yellow fluid, in order to save that in the canteen for a critical moment. Just then there was in front of us a terrific crashing, not like musketry, but more like the falling down of a thousand trees at once. Our brigade, a small one, was hurried into line of battle at the edge of an open field that sloped down a little in front of us and then up to a wood-covered ridge. That wood was full of the Rebel army. Fighting was going on to the right and left of us, and bullets flew into our own line, wounding some of us as we stood there waiting.

There was an old well and curb at the immediate right of my regiment, and many of our boys were climbing over each other to get a drop of water. Soon the bullets came faster, zipping, zipping among us, thicker and thicker. We must have been in full view of the enemy as we stood there, not firing a shot. Our line stood still in terrible suspense, not knowing why we were put under fire without directions to shoot. *Zip! zip! zip!* came the Rebel bullets, and now and then a boy in blue would groan, strike his hand to a wounded limb or arm, drop his gun and fall to the rear; or perhaps he fell in his tracks dead, without uttering a word. We too, who saw it, uttered no word, but watched steadily, anxiously at the front.

Then General Grant himself rode up behind us, and so close to the spot where I stood, that I could have heard his voice. He leaned against his little bay horse, had the inevitable cigar in his mouth, and was calm as a statue. Possibly smoking so much tranquillized his nerves a little and aided in producing calmness. Still, Grant was calm everywhere; but he also smoked everywhere. Be that as it may, it required very solid courage to stand there quietly behind that line at that moment. For my own part, I was in no agreeable state of mind. In short, I might be killed there at any moment, I thought, and I confess to having been nervous and alarmed. Every man in the line near me was looking serious, though determined. We had no reckless fools near us, whooping for blood. Once a badly wounded man was carried by the litter-bearers—the drummers of my regiment—close to the spot where the general stood. He gave a pitying glance at the man, I thought,—I was not twenty feet away,—but he neither spoke nor stirred.

Then I heard an officer say, "We are going to charge." It seems that our troops in front of us in the woods had been sadly repulsed, and now our division was to rush in and fight in their stead, and the commander-in-chief was there to witness our assault. Two or three of us, near each other, expressed dissatisfaction that the commander of an army in battle should expose himself, as General Grant was doing at that moment. When staff officers came up to him, he gave orders in low tones, and they would ride away. One of them, listening to him, glanced over our heads toward the Rebels awhile, looked very grave, and gave some mysterious nods. The colonel who was about to lead us also came to the general's side a moment. He, too, listened, looked, and gave some mysterious nods. Something was about to happen.

"My time has probably come now," I said to myself, and with a little bit of disgust I thought of the utter uselessness of being killed there without even firing a shot in self-defence. The suspense, the anxiety, was indeed becoming fearfully intense. Soon General Grant quietly climbed upon his horse, looked at us once, and as quietly rode away. Then the colonel came along the line with a word to each officer. As he came near me he called me from the ranks and said: "I want you to act as sergeant-major of the regiment in this battle." I was surprised, but indeed very proud of this mark of confidence in me. "Hurry to the left," he continued. "Order the men to fix bayonets—quick!"

I ran as told, shouting at the top of my voice, "Fix bayonets! fix bayonets!"

I was not quite to the left, when I heard other voices yelling, "Forward! quick! double quick! forward!" and the line was already on the run toward the Rebels.

I kept up my shouting, "Fix bayonets!" for by some blunder the order had not been given in time, and now the men were trying to get their bayonets in place while running. We were met in a minute by a storm of bullets from the wood, but the lines in blue kept steadily on, as would a storm of wind and cloud moving among the tree-tops. Now we met almost whole companies of wounded, defeated men from the other division, hurrying by us, and they held up their bleeding and mangled hands to show us they had not been cowards. They had lost twelve hundred men on the spot we were about to occupy.

Some of them were laughing even, and yelling at us: "Wade in and give them hell." We were wading in faster than I am telling the story.

On the edge of a low ridge we saw a solid wall of men in gray, their muskets at their shoulders blazing into our faces and their batteries of artillery roaring as if it were the end of the world. Bravely they stood there. They seemed little over a hundred yards away. There was no charging further by our line. We halted, the two lines stood still, and for over an hour we loaded our guns and killed each other as fast as we could. The firing and the noise were simply appalling. Now, I was not scared. The first shot I fired seemed to take all my fear away and gave me courage enough to calmly load my musket at the muzzle and fire it forty times. Others, with more cartridges, fired possibly oftener still. Some of the regiments in that bloody line were resupplied with cartridges from the boxes of the dead. In a moment I saw Captain Lindsey throw up his arms, spring upward and fall dead in his tracks. Corporal McCully was struck in the face by a shell. The blood covered him all over, but he kept on firing. Lieutenant Darling dropped dead, and other officers near me fell wounded.

I could not see far to left or right, the smoke of battle was covering everything. I saw bodies of our men lying near me without knowing who they were, though some of them were my messmates in the morning. The Rebels in front we could not see at all. We simply fired at their lines by guess, and occasionally the blaze of their guns showed exactly where they stood. They kept their line like a wall of fire. When I fired my first shot I had resolved to aim at somebody or something as long as I could see, and a dozen times I tried to bring down an officer I dimly saw on a gray horse before me. Pretty soon a musket ball struck me fair in the breast. "I am dead, now," I said, almost aloud. It felt as if someone had struck me with a club. I stepped back a few paces and sat down on a log to finish up with the world.

Other wounded men were there, covered with blood, and some were lying by me dead. I spoke to no one. It would have been useless; thunder could scarcely have been heard at that moment. My emotions I have almost forgotten. I remember only that something said to me, "It is honourable to die so." I had not a thought of friends, or of home, or of religion. The stupendous things going on around me filled my mind. On getting my breath a little I found I was not hurt at all,— simply stunned; the obliquely-fired bullet had struck the heavy leather of my cartridge belt and glanced away. I picked up my gun, stepped back into the line of battle, and in a moment was shot through the hand. The wound did not hurt; I was too excited for that.

The awful roar of battle now grew more terrific, if possible. I wonder that a man on either side was left alive. Biting the ends off my cartridges, my mouth was filled with gunpowder; the thirst was intolerable. Every soldier's face was black as a negro's, and, with some, blood from wounds trickled down over the blackness, giving them a horrible look. Once a boy from another part of the line to our left ran up to me crying out: "My regiment is gone! what shall I do?"

There was now a little moment's lull in the howling noise; something was going on. "Blaze away right here," I said to the boy, and he commenced firing like a veteran. Then I heard one of our own line cry, "My God, they're flanking us!" I looked to where the boy had come from. His regiment had indeed given way. The Rebels had poured through the gap and were already firing into our rear and yelling to us to surrender. In a moment we would be surrounded. It was surrender or try to get back past them. I ran like a racehorse,—so did the left of the regiment, amid a storm of bullets and yells and curses. I saved my musket, anyway. I think all did that,—but that half-mile race through a hot Mississippi sun, with bullets and cannonballs ploughing the fields behind us, will never be forgotten. My lungs seemed to be burning up. Once I saw our regimental flag lying by a log, the colour-bearer wounded or dead. I cried to a comrade flying near me, "Duncan Teter, it is a shame—the Fifth Iowa running."

Only the day before Teter had been reduced to the ranks for some offense or another. He picked up the flag and with a great oath dared me to stop and defend it. For a moment we two tried to rally to the flag the men who were running by. We might as well have yelled to a Kansas cyclone. Then Captain John Tait, rushing by, saw us, stopped, and, recognizing the brave deed of Corporal Teter, promoted him on the spot. But the oncoming storm was irresistible, and, carrying the flag, we all again hurried rearward. We had scarcely passed the spot where I had seen Grant mount his horse before the charge when a whole line of Union cannon, loaded to the muzzle with grape-shot and canister, opened on the howling mob that was pursuing us. The Rebels instantly halted, and now again it seemed our turn. A few minutes rest for breath and our re-formed lines once more dashed into the woods.

In half an hour the Battle of Champion Hills was won, and the victorious Union army was shortly in a position to compel the surrender of the key to the Mississippi River. Grant's crown of immortality was won, and the jewel that shone most brightly in it was set there by the blood of the men of Champion Hills. Had that important battle failed, Grant's army, not Pemberton's, would have become prisoners of war. Where then would have been Vicksburg, Spotsylvania, Richmond, Appomattox?

Six thousand blue- and gray-coated men were lying there in the woods, dead or wounded, when the last gun of Champion Hills was fired. Some of the trees on the battlefield were tall magnolias, and many of their limbs were shot away. The trees were in full bloom, their beautiful blossoms contrasting with the horrible scene of battle. Besides killing and wounding three thousand of the enemy, we had also captured thirty cannon and three thousand prisoners.

When the troops went off into the road to start in pursuit of the flying enemy, I searched over the battlefield for my best friend, poor Captain Poag, with whom I had talked of our Northern homes only the night before. He lay dead among the leaves, a bullet hole in his forehead. Somebody buried him, but I never saw his grave. Another friend I found dying. He begged me only to place him against a tree, and with leaves to shut the burning sun away from his face. While I was doing this I heard the groaning of a Rebel officer, who lay helpless in a little ditch. He called to me to lift him out, as he was shot through both thighs, and suffering terribly.

"Yes," I said, "as soon as I get my friend here arranged a little comfortably."

His reply was pathetic. "Yes, that's right; help your own first."

I had not meant it so. I instantly got to him and, with the aid of a comrade, pulled him out of the ditch. He thanked me and told me he was a lieutenant colonel, and had been shot while riding in front of the spot where he lay. I eased his position as best I could, but all that night, with many another wounded soldier, blue and gray, he was left on the desolate battlefield.

Now I realized how terrible the fire had been about us,—for some comrades counted two hundred bullet marks on a single oak tree within a few feet of where the left of the regiment had stood loading and firing that awful hour and a half. Most of the bullets had been fired too high, else we had all been killed. Nearby lay the remains of a Rebel battery. Every horse and most of the cannoneers lay dead in a heap, the caissons and the gun carriages torn to pieces by our artillery. Never in any battle had I seen such a picture of complete annihilation of men, animals, and material as was the wreck of this battery, once the pride of some Southern town—its young men, the loved ones of

Southern homes, lying there dead among their horses. That was war!

Some weeks after this battle, and after Vicksburg had been won, my regiment was marched in pursuit of Joe Johnston, and we recrossed this same battlefield. We reached it in the night and bivouacked on the very spot where we had fought. It was a strange happening. Our sensations were very unusual, for we realized that all about us there in the woods were the graves of our buried comrades and the still un-buried bones of many of our foes. Save an occasional hooting owl the woods were sad and silent. Before we lay down in the leaves to sleep the glee club of Company B sang that plaintive song, "We're Tenting Tonight on the Old Camp Ground." Never was a song sung under sadder circumstances.

All the night a terrible odour filled the bivouac. When daylight came one of the boys came to our company and said, "Go over to that hollow, and you will see hell." Some of us went. We looked but once. Dante himself never conjured anything so horrible as the reality before us. After the battle the Rebels in their haste had tossed hundreds of their dead into this little ravine and slightly covered them over with earth, but the rains had come, and the earth was washed away, and there stood or lay hundreds of half-decayed corpses. Some were grinning skeletons, some were headless, some armless, some had their clothes torn away, and some were mangled by dogs and wolves. The horror of that spectacle followed us for weeks. That, too, was war!

I have written this random but true sketch of personal recollections of a severe battle because it may help young men who are anxious for adventure and war, as I was, to first realize what war really is. My experiences probably were the same as hundreds of others in that same battle. I only tell of what was nearest me. A third of my comrades who entered this fight were lost. Other Iowa and other Western regiments suffered equally or more. General Hovey's division had a third of its number slain. I have been in what history pronounces greater battles than Champion Hills, but only once did I ever see two lines of blue and gray stand close together and fire into each other's faces for an hour and a half. I think the courage of the private soldiers, standing in that line of fire for that awful hour and a half, gave us Vicksburg, made Grant immortal as a soldier, and helped to save this country.

But I must return to that afternoon of the battle. All that could be assembled of our men gathered in line in a road near the field. It was nearly dark. Sergeant Campbell walked about, making a list of the dead and wounded of Company B. As I was not now on the company rolls, being quartermaster sergeant, my name was not put down as one of the wounded. Nor, seeing how many were sadly torn to pieces, did I think my wound worth reporting.

Shortly General Grant passed us in the road. Knowing well how the regiment had fought in the battle, he rode to where our colours hung over a stack of muskets and saluted them. We all jumped to our feet and cheered. He spoke a few words to the colonel and rode on into the darkness. That night we marched ahead, and in the morning bivouacked in the woods as a reserve for troops fighting at the Black River bridge. *There it was that Grant reached the crisis of his career.* While sitting on his horse waiting to witness a charge by Lawler's brigade, a staff officer overtook him, bringing a peremptory order from Washington to *abandon the campaign* and take his army to Port Hudson to help General Banks.

That moment Grant glanced to the right of his lines and saw a dashing officer in his shirt sleeves suddenly come out of a cluster of woods, leading his brigade to the assault. It was General Lawler, and in five minutes the Rebel breastworks were carried, the enemy in flight or drowning in the rapid river. Then Grant turned to the staff officer and simply said, "*See that charge! I think it is too late to abandon this campaign.*" The movements that were to make him immortal went on. Had that order of Halleck's, written of course without knowledge of the recent victories, been followed, Banks, and not Grant, would have been first commander in the West. Had Lawler's charge failed just then and the battle been lost, Grant could have had no excuse for not obeying the order that staff officer held in his hand, directing him to abandon what turned out to be one of the great campaigns of history. While sitting there in his saddle at the close of that charge, General Grant wrote a little note in pencil, the original of which is among my treasured souvenirs of the war:

Dear General: Lawler's brigade stormed the enemy's works a few minutes since; carried them, capturing from two thousand to three thousand prisoners, ten guns, so far as heard from, and probably more will be found. The enemy have fired both bridges. A. J. Smith captured ten guns this morning, with teams, men, and ammunition. I send you a note from Colonel Wright.
Yours,
U. S. Grant, M. G.

To Major General Sherman.

CHAPTER 8

Assaults on the Walls of Vicksburg

The next morning (the 18th) my regiment crossed the pontoon bridge over the Big Black and marched eight miles further toward Vicksburg. Now we knew we were getting close to the Richmond of the West. As we crossed the Black River we gazed with curiosity at the half-burned bridge from which so many unfortunates had been hurled into the water by our artillery the day before. After Lawler's charge thousands had tried to get over the stream by the trestle-work and bridge, or by swimming. General Osterhaus, seeing the fugitives from a high point where he stood, cried out to his batteries: "Now, men, is the time to give them hell." Twenty cannon instantly hurled their iron missiles at the bridge, and the flying soldiers fell to the ground or into the foaming river, almost by hundreds. "Lost at Black River," was the only message that ever reached the home of many a Southern soldier of that day.

On the 19th, at two o'clock, a terrible assault was made by the army on the walls of Vicksburg. My own regiment, still in McPherson's corps, lay close to the Jackson wagon road and under a tremendous thundering of the enemy's artillery. We suffered little, however. Once I was ordered to help some men build sheds of brush for the wounded. This was in a ravine behind us. In an hour the work was done, and as I crept up the slope to get forward to my regiment again I heard the loud voice of some officer on horseback. It was General John A. Logan. The enemy's artillery was sweeping the field at this point, but I could still hear Logan's voice above the battle, cheering a number of soldiers that were near.

"We have taken this fort and we have taken that," he cried in tones that were simply stentorian. "We are giving them hell everywhere." He was in full uniform, his long black hair swept his shoulders, his

50

eyes flashed fire, he seemed the incarnation of the reckless, fearless soldier. He must have thought cannonballs would not hurt him. For five minutes, perhaps, I stood in a little dip in the ground, comparatively protected, while he rode up and down under a storm of cannonballs, calling at the top of his warrior's voice. I expected every moment to see him drop from his horse, but nothing happened, and I went on to the line where all our men were closely hugging the ground. Soon I, too, was stretched on the ground, making myself as thin as I could.

On the 20th we advanced still closer to the frowning works. It was only a thousand yards to the forts of Vicksburg. We moved up in the darkness that night. I think no one knew how close we were being taken to the enemy. We lay down in line of battle and in the night our line was moved a little. When daylight came my regiment was no little astonished to find that we were on an open place in full view of the enemy. A comrade and I rose from the ground and commenced our toilet, by pouring water into each other's hands from our canteens. Almost at that moment the Rebels had caught sight of our men lying there in long lines so close to them, and instantly commenced throwing shells at us.

My friend and I left our morning toilet uncompleted and, seizing our rifles, we all stood in line waiting. We could see the flags of the enemy above the forts distinctly. With a glass the gunners could be seen at their guns, hurling shot and shell at us. We were in a perilous and helpless position. We were also very tired and hungry, for we had had nothing whatever to eat. But here we stayed, and by the next morning our skirmishers had advanced so close to the Vicksburg forts that the Rebel gunners could reach us but little. Our gunboats too, down in the river now commenced hurling mighty bombs and balls into the city.

On the morning of the 22nd of May all the batteries of the army and the big guns of the river fleet bombarded the city for an hour, and under the fog and the smoke of the battle the infantry advanced to assault the works. It was a perilous undertaking. The day was fearfully hot; the forts, ten feet high, were many and powerful; the ditches in front of them were seven feet deep. That made seventeen feet to climb in the face of musketry. In battle line, my regiment ran down into the ravines in front and then up the opposite slope to the smoking breastwork.

The colonel had ordered me to fasten two ammunition boxes across a mule and follow the regiment into the assault. I was to lead my mule. A soldier with a bush was to beat him from behind, so as to hurry him over an exposed bit of ground at our front. The moment my mule appeared in full sight of the enemy the bullets commenced whizzing past us. The mule, true to his ancestral instinct, commenced pulling backward. Yelling and pounding and pulling helped none at all. Two or three bullets struck the boxes on his back, and before we had pulled him half across he braced himself, held his ears back, and stood stock still. That moment the bridle came off. My assistant dodged back to our rifle pit and I hurried down to the ravine in front. The mule, too, as luck would have it, also ran now,—ran down into the ravine beside me, right where he was wanted. I tied him to a little bush and, awful as the situation about me was, I almost laughed to see the antics of that animal's ears as the bullets whizzed past him.

My regiment was all lying against the hill close up to the fort. In front of them was the ditch seven feet deep, beyond them an armed fort ten feet high, emitting a constant blaze of cannon and musketry. The sun was broiling hot. I crept along the line of the regiment and gave ammunition to every company; then I crept back a little to where my mule was still alive and his ears still at their antics. Lying there in the line beside the boys, roasting in the sun and suffering from the musketry in front, was our brave Colonel Boomer, leading the brigade. He asked me once what I was doing, and, when I told him, he gave me some compliments in a kind, but sad, low tone.

Now I saw a company of men creep by me, dragging little ladders in their hands. They were to make a rush and throw these ladders across the ditch of the forts for the assaulters to cross on. They were all volunteers for a work that seemed sure death. I looked in each hero's face as he passed me, knowing almost that he would be dead in a few minutes. Scarcely a dozen of them returned alive. My regiment, with the rest of the assaulters, was simply being shot to pieces without a hope of getting into the forts. We fell back under the smoke of the battle as best we could, only to be led into an assault at another point. McClernand had sent Grant word that he had taken a fort on our left. He wanted help to hold it.

Our division, now led by Quimby, was double-quicked to the next place of assault. I saved my mule. Again I strapped two ammunition boxes over his back and followed the regiment. This time I did not risk my mule so close in the battle, but took all the cartridges I could carry in my arms and went to the left of the regiment. Once I saw a body lying on the grass by me, with a handkerchief over the face. I went up and looked. It was our own Colonel Boomer, who had spoken so kindly to me in the morning. A useless charge had already been made by the brigade and he, with many brave men, was dead. Some of my own company lay dead there too. One of them had come from Iowa and joined his brother in the company that very morning. All the assaulting of the 22nd of May and all the sacrifice of life had been for nothing. Vicksburg was not taken.

Now commenced the regular siege of the city. We hid ourselves behind ridges, in hollows, and in holes in the ground, as best we could. Communication with our gunboats on the Yazoo was opened, and we had plenty to eat and ammunition enough to bombard a dozen cities. Then the bombardment commenced indeed, and lasted to the end, forty-four days. We often threw three hundred cannonballs and shells a day into the city. The whole Rebel army was also hidden in holes and hollows. All the people of Vicksburg lived in caves at the sides of the hills or along the bluffs of the river. Their homes now were like swallows' nests, with small entrances in the face of hills and bluffs and big, dugout chambers inside. It was a strange life. With the eternal hail of cannon over them day and night, and starvation a familiar figure to them, it must have been a horrible one.

Now we advanced our rifle pits and trenches and mines close up to the Rebel forts, though our main lines lay in the ravines and on the ridge a few hundred feet farther back. As for me, when not looking after the ammunition, a trifling duty now, I was in the trenches with the others.

One morning when out there at the front among our riflemen, who were forever blazing day and night at every Rebel fort and rifle pit, I noticed our good Colonel Matthies creeping along the trench to where I was. He had a package of brown paper in his hand. Imagine my surprise and pride to have him come to me and say: "Sergeant, this officer's sash is yours." Then he announced my appointment as adjutant of the regiment. He had been made a general now, and would soon leave for his new command. This sash was one that he had worn and honoured on many a battlefield. Is it any wonder that now, after the long and perilous years, it is preserved by me as a souvenir of honour?

Soon after, I went to a sutler's store on the Yazoo River to buy a sword and uniform. In those days swords were not given to officers by committees in dress coats, until they had been earned. This little trip to get my sword almost cost me my life. My path to the river, six miles away, lay partly along a ridge and partly close to an empty Rebel fort. This fort showed scarcely any signs of having ever been used. I stayed all night with the sutler, whom I knew very well, and at noon on a hot day started, on my big yellow government horse, to go back to my regiment. My sword was buckled on me and my new uniform was tied in a bundle on my saddle-bow. It was too hot to ride fast, and my horse almost slept as he slowly carried me close by the seemingly abandoned fort. Suddenly there was a crash and a whole volley of musketry rattled about my ears.

My poor horse fell dead. It was a quick awakening, but I managed to pull my bundle from the saddle-bow and to escape into a ravine where our own troops lay. There I learned that the fort had been occupied by the Rebels in the night, while I was with the sutler. It was a close call for me. One of the boys declared he could save my saddle and bridle. "Take them as a present," I said, "if you can get them." He crept up to where my dead horse lay, and as he rose to his feet to undo the saddle another volley from the fort hastened him to the ravine. I laughed. "If your saddle and bridle were made of gold and silver," he shouted at me as he ran back, "I wouldn't try it again."

Slowly and without perceptible advance the siege went on. The little battery that my regiment had saved at Iuka was still with us and behind some breastworks at our immediate right. It was no uncommon thing to see even Grant himself come along and stop and watch Captain Sears' guns knock the dirt up from some fort in front of us. One day this battery wounded a man who was running between two Rebel breastworks. The enemy tried to secure his body, but every soul that showed himself for an instant was shot by our riflemen. For half an hour this shooting over one poor man's body was kept up, until it seemed that a battle was taking place.

Now our lines were so close together that our pickets often had a cup of coffee or a chew of tobacco with the Rebel pickets at night. Drummer Bain, of my company, had a brother among the soldiers inside Vicksburg. One night he met him at the picket line, and together they walked all through the beleaguered town. But such things were dangerous business and had to be kept very quiet. The weather was now very warm and fine, some of the nights clear moonlight, and when the guns had stopped their roaring many a time in the quiet night we heard the bell clock on the Vicksburg Court House measuring out the hours. It is said that this clock never stopped for an instant in all the siege, nor under the hundred cannon that rained iron hail into the town. At night, too, the big mortars from our fleet some miles from us tossed mighty bombs into the air, that sailed like blazing comets and fell at last among the people hidden in their caves.

One day Governor Kirkwood of Iowa visited our regiment and made a speech to us in a hollow back of our line. We cheered, and the Rebels, hearing us and knowing we must be assembled in masses, hurled a hundred cannonballs and shells over our heads, yet I think few were hurt. This was the 3rd of June. Every night that we lay there on the line we went to sleep fearing to be waked by an attack from the army of Rebels under Johnston, now assembled at our rear. This was the force we most feared, not the army we had penned up in Vicksburg. Nevertheless, the batteries in front of us gave us enough to do to prevent any ennui on our part. On the 15th of June the enemy got one big gun in a position to rake from our left the ravine in which my regiment was lying. We all stuck close to our little caves on the ridge side, and few got hurt. In the meantime we were working day and night putting more breastworks in front of us, though we were now but four hundred yards away from the Rebel lines. Here, as many times elsewhere, I copy from my diary:

> Last night, the 16th, the major of our regiment, Marshall, took two hundred men and worked all night digging new ditches and building breastworks. It was rainy and muddy. The Rebels heard us at the work and in the darkness slipped up and captured a few men. Some of the enemy, however, also got taken in. This is the kind of work that is going on every night until daybreak, and then we fire bullets all the day into the enemy's lines, to prevent their repairing their forts. The cannonading and the rifle shooting never cease. The roar is simply incessant, and yet when off duty we sleep like newborn babes.
>
> All the region we are in is hills and ravines, brush and canebrake, with here and there a little cotton field. Nature defends Vicksburg more than a dozen armies could. She has built scores of positions around the town strong as anything at Sevastapol.

The rumours kept coming of a purposed attack on our rear. On the 20th of June, at four o'clock in the morning, all the cannon on Grant's lines and all the cannon on the gunboats opened fire on the town and thundered at it for six mortal hours. They must have been awful hours for the people inside. No such cannonading ever took place on the continent before or since. We private soldiers did not know the exact object of this fearful bombardment. The Rebels probably lay in battle line, expecting an assault, and must have suffered greatly

In the night of the 22nd of June, at midnight, rumours again came of a great Rebel army marching on our rear. It was a beautiful moonlight night, and my regiment, together with whole divisions of the army, received orders to hurry back toward Black River, where cavalry skirmishing had taken place. No battle came on, but for two days we lay in line of battle, or else built breastworks for defence.

On the 3rd of July, as we were bivouacked in a little wood, news came that the whole Rebel army in Vicksburg had prepared to surrender the next day, the Nation's jubilee day. Instantly the regiment was ordered to fall in. I had no little pride in reading to the men the dispatch from General Grant announcing the great news. It was the first order I had ever read to the regiment as its adjutant, and its great importance gratified me much. The whole command acted as if they were drunken or had suddenly lost their minds. Privates and officers shook hands and laughed and wept, while majors and colonels turned somersaults on the grass. It was indeed a great moment to us all. Twenty-seven thousand men, with twenty-four generals and one hundred and eighty cannon, was a great capture. We all knew we had made history on that day.

Now the whole Rebel army passed out along the roads where we lay. I sat on a rail fence near our bivouac and watched the host go by. The officers all looked depressed, but the soldiers seemed glad the suspense and danger were over and that now they could have enough to eat. Our regiment freely divided with them all we had.

After a few days pursuit of Johnston's army at our rear (now suddenly our front), my regiment is ordered into Vicksburg. We pass in over the breastworks that had been so terrible to us a few days before. Looking at them, I wonder at our hardihood in assaulting them. It would be hard to climb through these ditches and into these forts even were no cannon and no deadly muskets behind them.

My regiment is put on duty as a city guard. It now seems strange enough to be guarding the very town and the very forts we had so recently been assaulting. There are other troops here, but the Fifth Iowa is the guard proper. We find the town badly battered up, with terrible signs of war everywhere. There, too, were the graves of the dead and brave defenders. If wrong, they still had been brave men.

Years afterward, a shaft was put up to their memory, and on it I read these words:

We care not whence they came,
Dear in their lifeless clay,
Whether unknown, or known to fame,
Their cause and country's still the same,
They died, and they wore the gray.

The weather continued hot while we were there guarding the town, and the place was very sickly; many citizens and very many coloured soldiers died. It was pitiable to see how little people cared, even our own soldiers, whether these poor negro soldiers died or lived. Our own regiment suffered little, yet on July 28 seventy were in the hospital. We camped at Randolph and Locust streets, and spite of the mercury's being 100 degrees in the shade, had pleasant soldier times. I mounted the guard every morning and then spent most of the day reading to the colonel, who was sick.

In September I secured a leave of absence to go North. For the only time during the four years' war I visited my home. I was there but eight days, half of my time having been lost by the steamer I was on sticking on sandbars.

I saw strange sights in the North in those few days—women and children and old men reaping the fields; home guards training at every village; cripples and hospitals everywhere. Yet in spite of war prosperity was blessing the North.

CHAPTER 9

My Capture

On my return from my home to my regiment I found it had been transported to Memphis, where, as a part of General Sherman's army corps, we were now to make a forced march to relieve Rosecrans' army at Chattanooga. Chickamauga had been lost. The Union army lying under Lookout Mountain was starving and its destruction almost certain. We made now the march of four hundred miles from the Tennessee River, at Florence, in twenty days, without incident. On the 22nd of November, 1863, we beheld the heights of Lookout Mountain and Missionary Ridge.

November 23, 1863, and the great Battle of Chattanooga was about to begin. The victorious Rebel army, seventy-five thousand strong, lay intrenched along the heights of Missionary Ridge and on top of Lookout Mountain. My regiment was in Sherman's corps that had just hurried across from Memphis. We had marched twenty miles a day. Now this corps was to form the left of Grant's forces, cross a deep river in the darkness, and assault the nearly inaccessible position of Bragg's army. That night we lay in bivouac in the woods close by the Tennessee River. We very well knew that 116 rude pontoon boats had been built for us and were lying hidden in a creek nearby. We had almost no rations for the army.

As for the horses and mules, they had already starved to death by the thousands, and were lying around everywhere. Rosecran's army had been virtually besieged, and was about to starve or surrender when Grant came on to the ground and took command. When Sherman's corps got up it was decided to stake all on a great battle. If defeated, we should probably all be lost. All the men in Sherman's corps who were to make the first great assault realized that, and they realized also the danger we were now to encounter by attempting to cross that rapid river in the night.

Midnight came and all were still awake, though quiet in the bivouac. At two o'clock we heard some quiet splashing in the water. It
was the sound of muffled oars. The boats had come for us. Every man
seized his rifle, for we knew what was coming next. "Quietly, boys, fall
in quietly," said the captains. Spades were handed to many of us. We
did not ask for what, as we knew too well. Quietly, two by two, we
slipped down to the water's edge and stepped into the rude flatboats
that waited there. "Be prompt as you can, boys; there's room for thirty
in a boat," said a tall man in a long waterproof coat who stood on
the bank near us in the darkness. Few of us had ever before heard the
voice of our beloved commander. Sherman's kind words gave us all
cheer, and his personal presence, his sharing the danger we were about
to undertake, gave us confidence.

In a quarter of an hour a thousand of us were out in the middle of
the river afloat in the darkness. Silent we sat there, our rifles and our
spades across our knees. There was no sound but the swashing of the
water against the boats. We had strange feelings, the chief of which
was probably the thought: Would the enemy on the opposite bank
fire into us and drown us all? Every moment we expected a flash of
musketry or a roar of cannon. We did not know that a ruse had been
played on the pickets on the other side; that a boatload of our soldiers
had crossed farther up and in the darkness caught every one of them
without firing a shot. One only got away. Who knew how soon all of
Braggs' army might be alarmed and upon us?

In half an hour we were out on the opposite bank and creeping
along through the thicket, a spade in one hand a rifle in the other.
What might happen any moment we knew not. Where was that escaped picket? And where was Braggs' army? Instantly we formed in
line of battle and commenced digging holes for ourselves. We worked
like beavers, turn about; no spade was idle for one moment. Daylight
found us there, two thousand strong, with rifle pits a mile in length.
Other brigades got over the river, pontoons soon were down; still other troops, whole divisions, were across, and forty cannon were massed
close to the crossing to protect us. What a sight was that for General
Bragg, when he woke up that morning at his headquarters' perch, on
top of Missionary Ridge! All that day we manoeuvred under heavy
cannonading and drove the enemy from hill to hill at our front. Some
of the troops did heavy fighting, but the Rebels only fell back to their
great position on the Ridge.

That night my regiment stood picket at the front. The ground was cold and wet, none of us slept a wink, and we were almost freezing and starving. We had not slept, indeed, for a hundred hours. It had been one vast strain, and now a battle was coming on. All that night we who were on the picket line could hear the Rebel field batteries taking position on Missionary Ridge, to fight us on the morrow. The morning of the 25th dawned clear and beautiful. Instantly whole divisions of troops commenced slaughtering each other for the possession of single hills and spurs. At times the battle in front of Sherman was a hand to hand encounter. My own brigade was so close that the Rebels even threw stones down upon us. Over to the far right Hooker's men were in possession of Lookout Mountain, and were breaking in on the enemy's left flank.

It was two o'clock when our division, my own regiment with it, received orders from Sherman to fix bayonets and join in the assault on Missionary Ridge. General J. E. Smith led the division, and General Matthies, our former colonel, led the brigade. We had to charge over the open, and by this time all the cannon in the Rebel army were brought to bear on the field we had to cross. We emerged from a little wood, and at that moment the storm of shot and shell became terrific. In front of us was a rail fence, and, being in direct line of fire, its splinters and fragments flew in every direction. "Jump the fence, men! tear it down!" cried the colonel. Never did men get over a fence more quickly. Our distance was nearly half a mile to the Rebel position.

We started on a charge, running across the open fields. I had heard the roaring of heavy battle before, but never such a shrieking of cannonballs and bursting of shell as met us on that charge. We could see the enemy working their guns, while in plain view other batteries galloped up, unlimbered, and let loose at us. Behind us our own batteries (forty cannon) were firing at the enemy over our heads, till the storm and roar became horrible. It sounded as if the end of the world had come. Halfway over we had to leap a ditch, perhaps six feet wide and nearly as many deep. Some of our regiment fell into this ditch and could not get out, a few tumbled in intentionally and stayed there. I saw this, and ran back and ordered them to get out, called them cowards, threatened them with my revolver; they did not move.

Again I hurried on with the line. All of the officers were screaming at the top of their voices; I, too, screamed, trying to make the men hear. "Steady! steady! bear to the right! keep in line! Don't fire! don't fire!" was yelled till we all were hoarse and till the awful thunder of the cannon made all commands unheard and useless.

In ten minutes, possibly, we were across the field and at the beginning of the ascent of the Ridge. Instantly the blaze of Rebel musketry was in our faces, and we began firing in return. It helped little, the foe was so hidden behind logs and stones and little breastworks. Still we charged, and climbed a fence in front of us and fired and charged again. Then the order was given to lie down and continue firing. That moment someone cried, "Look to the tunnel! They're coming through the tunnel." Sure enough, through a railway tunnel in the mountain the gray-coats were coming by hundreds. They were flanking us completely.

"Stop them!" cried our colonel to those of us at the right. "Push them back." It was but the work of a few moments for four companies to rise to their feet and run to the tunnel's mouth, firing as they ran. Too late! an enfilading fire was soon cutting them to pieces. "Shall I run over there too?" I said to the colonel. We were both kneeling on the ground close to the regimental flag. He assented. When I rose to my feet and started it seemed as if even the blades of grass were being struck by bullets. As I ran over I passed many of my comrades stretched out in death, and some were screaming in agony. For a few minutes the whole brigade faltered and gave way.

Colonel Matthies, our brigade commander, was sitting against a tree, shot in the head. Instantly it seemed as if a whole Rebel army was concentrated on that single spot. For a few moments I lay down on the grass, hoping the storm would pass over and leave me. Lieutenant Miller, at my side, was screaming in agony. He was shot through the hips. I begged him to try to be still; he could not. Now, as a second line of the enemy was upon us, and the first one was returning, shooting men as they found them, I rose to my feet and surrendered. "Come out of that sword," shrieked a big Georgian, with a terrible oath. Another grabbed at my revolver and bellowed at me "to get up the hill quicker than hell." It was time, for our own batteries were pouring a fearful fire on the very spot where we stood. I took a blanket from a dead comrade near me, and at the point of the bayonet I was hurried up the mountain. We passed lines of infantry in rifle pits and batteries that were pouring a hail of shells into our exposed columns. Once I glanced back, and—glorious sight!—I saw lines of bluecoats at our right and centre, storming up the ridge.

In a few minutes' time I was taken to where other prisoners from my regiment and brigade were already collected together in a hollow. We were quickly robbed of nearly everything we possessed and rapidly

61

started down the railroad tracks toward Atlanta. While we were there in that little hollow General Breckenridge, the ex-Vice President of the United States, came in among us prisoners to buy a pair of Yankee gauntlets. I sold him mine for fifteen dollars (Confederate money).

General Grant's victorious army was already over the Ridge and in rapid pursuit. Taking the Ridge and Lookout Mountain cost the Union army well on to six thousand dead and wounded. The Rebels lost as many, or more, so that twelve thousand human beings were lying dead, or in agony, that night among the hills of Chattanooga. Not long before, thirty thousand had been killed and wounded, on both sides, close to this same Ridge. Forty-two thousand men shot for the possession of a single position. *That was war.*

That night as the guards marched us down the railroad we saw train after train whiz by loaded with the wounded of the Rebel army. The next day when they halted us, to bivouac in the woods, we were amazed to see quite a line of Union men from East Tennessee marching along in handcuffs. Many of them were old men, farmers, whose only crime was that they were true to the Union. They were hated ten times worse than the soldiers from the North. These poor men now were allowed no fire in the bivouac, and had almost nothing to eat. "They will everyone be shot or hanged," declared the officer of our guard to me. I do not know what happened to these poor Tennesseans. Shortly after, we Northern prisoners were put aboard cattle cars and started off for Libby Prison at Richmond, most of us never to see the North or our homes again.

CHAPTER 9

In Libby Prison

The story of Libby Prison at Richmond has been told so often I shall not dwell on details about it here. Besides, the experiences of one man there were not materially different from the experiences of another. I was to stay there some seven months, always in the same room, and oftenest denied the poor privilege of looking out of the window. Our lives were to be very wretched there. That is now a thread-worn tale. At their very best, war prisons in every country are wretched places. One's friends do not stand guard there; it is our enemies. They are not penal establishments; they are simply places for keeping captives who, until in our so-called civilized days, would have been put to death on the battlefield.

Our little company of captives from Chattanooga reached Libby Prison just after daylight of December 8, 1863. As we crossed the big bridge over the James River we looked down into the stream and saw "Belle Isle." It was a cold wet sandbar, and there, shivering in the wind, we saw five thousand ragged and emaciated human beings. They were prisoners of war. Some of them were from my own regiment. Most of them were never to see their homes again. The tales of their experiences would stagger human belief. These were all private soldiers; the commissioned officers were to be locked up in Libby Prison.

The old tobacco warehouse of Libby & Son had been transformed into a monster guardhouse for officers captured from the Federal army. Little the two old tobacco merchants must have dreamed with what infamy their names would go down to history, through no fault of their own.

The big brick building stood close to the James River. It had no glass in its windows, and the cold wind from the bay swept through its vast rooms day and night. Six hundred other prisoners were already there on our arrival, picked up from many battlefields.

Libby Prison was three stories high and its floors were divided into several rooms each. The prisoners slept on the floor, with only old army blankets around them. When thus lying down, the floor was entirely covered with shivering human beings. Each group of half a dozen men had extemporized tables, made from old boxes. A few seats were made by cutting barrels in two. At night the seats, and whatever else might be there, were piled on top of the tables, while the prisoners stretched themselves on the floor to try to sleep. In my diary of the time I read:

> The food doled out to us is miserable and scanty in the extreme. A species of corn bread, ground up cobs and all, and a little rice form the principal part of the ration. The fact that this bread is burned black outside and is raw inside renders it more detestable. Occasionally letters from the North reach us by a flag of truce, and at very rare intervals a prisoner is allowed to receive a little box of coffee, sugar, and salt, sent to him by his friends in the North.

As the time went on this privilege was denied us. The high price of everything South in the war times was the flimsy excuse for giving the captured ones so little.

Prices of provisions were indeed terrible in Richmond. This list I copied from a Richmond paper, December 20, 1863: Bacon, $3 per pound; potatoes, $18 per bushel; turkeys, $25 each; sugar, $3 per pound; beef, $1 per pound; butter, $5 per pound; shad, $34 per pair; whisky, $75 a gallon. This was in the discounted money of the Confederates.

The beginning of the new year 1864 came in cold and gloomy. We could keep warm only by running and jumping and pushing each other about the prison. I was in the upper east room, and had for messmates Captains Page and Bascom and Lieutenants Austin and Hoffman, all of my own regiment. In the little box of provisions sent me by my mother in the North was a copy of a Latin grammar, put there by good old Professor Drake, my former schoolteacher. Evidently he thought the mind needed feeding as well as the body. I took the hint and studied the book faithfully. I recited to Major Marshall, and eight times I went through this Latin grammar. I had nothing else to do, but Latin is no go on an empty stomach. When, later, I got out of prison Latin was as strange to me as if I had never seen a grammar in my life.

My memory had been well-nigh ruined by my confinement. One day, fearing our escape, the authorities put iron bars on all our windows. They did not think to put glass in them to keep the cold air out.

On the night of February 10 occurred the famous escape of one hundred and nine prisoners. For many weeks certain officers had been missing. They were in the earth under the prison, digging a tunnel to liberty. The length of this secret tunnel, dug under the prison, under stone walls, under the street and under the very feet of the guards, was eighty-six feet.

Forty-six nights were consumed in digging it. Only certain of the prisoners knew anything about it. On the night of the escape I was told of it. I stood in the dark at an upper window and watched the prisoners as they came out at the farther end of the tunnel and slipped away. I did not try to enter the tunnel when I heard of it; there was already five times as many men in the cellar as could possible get away by daylight. As it was, a third of those escaping were captured and brought back again to the prison.

On the 20th of March some exchanged Confederates were sent into Richmond under flag of truce. The President, Jefferson Davis, and all the dignitaries welcomed them. The President also came into Libby Prison one day, possibly to see with his own eyes and hear with his own ears if all the terrible tales of hardship and cruelties occurring there were true. Whatever conclusion he may have reached, the hard lines of our life in the prison were not visibly altered. They have been told of a hundred of times.

All the nights now it was very cold. I had but one blanket. I, like all the others, slept on the floor, and in my clothes, with my boots under my head for a pillow. One night,—it was at the close of February, 1864,—we in the prison were greatly excited over a report that Union cavalry under Generals Kilpatrick and Dahlgren were making a raid on the city for the purpose of releasing us. It was raining outside, and very dark, but we were sure we heard the Union cannon close at hand. We thought the hour of our deliverance had come. Instantly, but secretly, we organized ourselves into bands to break out and help.

Soon Major Turner, the prison commander, came into the prison, making mysterious threats of something awful that would happen should we lift a single hand. Some negro help about the prison whispered to us all that, under Turner's direction, they had been compelled to carry thirty kegs of gunpowder into the cellar of the prison. Rumour said that it was Turner's intention, if our troops should get into

65

Richmond, to blow up the prison and destroy us. A horrible plan, if true. Sadly for us, the great raid proved a failure. Dahlgren was killed, and his body was mutilated and exposed to an enraged public at one of the railroad depots in the city. These things were not done by honourable Confederate soldiers, but by irresponsible home guards and undisciplined rowdies.

Now we saw no hopes of ever getting away. We would at last all die here, we thought. The nights seemed colder than ever; perhaps our blood was getting thinner. Some of us played chess; numbers sat with cards in their hands from early morning till bedtime. A few, experts with the knife, made bone rings and the like to sell, and so increased their rations a little. Generally now the rations were getting poorer, if such a thing were possible. Many prisoners were breaking down and were carried out to die. My own health—and I was young and strong—was beginning to give way. Once I fell on the floor in an utter swoon from weakness and hunger. From Andersonville, where the private soldiers were, came the horrible reports that "all were dying."

One day a lot of Marylanders, most of whom had run through the Union lines from Baltimore, were organized into a battalion called "The Maryland Line." They were led by Marshall Wilder. They were marched past the prison, singing "Maryland, My Maryland." It was the first time I ever heard the song sung by Southerners. The music seemed to stir the whole city.[1]

Great battles were being fought in Virginia, and sometimes Grant's soldiers approached close to Richmond. Before daylight of May 7 our captors, fearing mutiny and escape, placed all the prisoners in cattle cars and hurried us across the Confederacy to Macon, Ga. For seven long, dreary, awful months I had been in one room in Libby Prison, with little to eat or wear. It all seems a horrible dream as I write of it now.

Now there were rumours that we were to be taken to a prison farther South.

---

1. Years afterwards I wrote a song to this music myself ("The Song of Iowa"). To this day, (as at time of first publication), it is well known, and has become the official State song.

CHAPTER 11

Escaping From Macon

I have related how suddenly we prisoners were hurried from Libby Prison in Richmond to the town of Macon in Georgia.

It was now the hot summer of 1864, that summer when Sherman, only a hundred and fifty miles from our prison, was having a battle every day. He was marching and fighting his way to Atlanta. Seven hundred of us, all Federal officers, were now penned up in a hot stockade. I copy a page from my diary:

"The walls here at Macon prison are twelve feet high. Sentries are posted near the top of them on a platform running around the outside. Their orders are to shoot any prisoners seen approaching the dead line. This dead line is simply marked off by an occasional stake, and is twelve feet inside the surrounding wall. It is fearfully hot here inside this stockade. The ground is pure sand, reflecting the sun's rays powerfully. We had no cover of any kind at first, save the blankets stretched over pine sticks. It is as hot here at Macon as it was cold at Libby Prison."

We tried digging a tunnel by which to escape. It was four feet under ground and seventy-five feet long. It was barely ready when some spy revealed it, and our chance was lost. For my own part, I was determined to get away. The food was now again horrible, and all kinds of indignities and insults were heaped upon the prisoners. One night during a hard rain I attempted to escape through a washout under the stockade. I remained by the spot till nearly midnight, not knowing that I was being watched every moment. As I was about to give up the attempt and go away Captain Gesner, of a New York regiment, came to the little brook for a cup of water. The guard who had been watching me then fired, and Gesner dropped dead. They came in with lanterns to see who had been killed, and the guard who had fired related how he had watched the man for nearly two hours trying to escape. I did not dare say that it was I, not poor Gesner, who had been trying to get away.

Now I contemplated, too, a different means of escape. It was to get a Rebel uniform, escape from the stockade by some means, and enter the Rebel army in disguise, trusting my chance to get away during the first battle.

There was but one gate or door to the stockade, and this door was kept constantly closed. It was guarded by a sentinel who stood, gun in hand, immediately above it while a corporal stood watch below. Once a day a few guards and officers entered this door, closed it behind them, and formed us into lines for counting. I had studied a small map of the country for days, and by dint of trading tobacco, etc., with an occasional guard who was dying for the weed I acquired, piece by piece, a pretty decent Rebel uniform. This I kept buried in the sand where I slept. July 15, 1864, came around. My term of enlistment expired that day. I had been in the Union army three years; was it not a good time to give the Rebels a trial? There were a few old sheds not far from the gate, and in one of these one morning about nine o'clock I waited with a friend, and saw the sergeants and the guards come in, when the bell rang, to count the prisoners. I had resurrected my Rebel uniform and had quietly slipped it on. It fitted amazingly. My friend was lingering there, simply to see what would become of me. He has often declared since then that he expected me to be shot the moment I should approach the dead-line.

The prisoners were some way off, in rows, being counted. I stepped from under cover and quickly walked up to and over the dead-line by the gate. The guard walking above brought his gun from his shoulder, halted, and looked at me. I paid no attention, but knocked, when the door opened, and the corporal stepped in the opening and asked what I wanted. "The lieutenant misses a roll-list, and I must run out and bring it from headquarters," I answered, pushing by him hurriedly. There was no time for questions, and the corporal, before getting over his surprise, had passed me out as a Rebel sergeant. I quickly turned the corner, passed a number of "Johnnies" sitting on the grass drinking coffee and went straight up to the commandant's tent, near the edge of the wood, but did not go in. I had not looked behind me once, but expected every moment to hear a bullet whizzing after me. I passed behind the tent, walked slowly into the wood, and then ran my best for an hour.

I was outside of prison. How free, how green, how beautiful all things seemed! It was the joy of years in a few minutes. Of course I was instantly missed at the roll-call, and bloodhounds were soon upon my track. I avoided them, however, by different manoeuvres. I changed my course, shortly repassed the prison pen on the opposite side, and went back and up into the city of Macon. After wandering through its streets for an hour I again took to the woods. That night I slept in a swamp of the Ocmulgee River. What bedfellows I had!—frogs, lizards, bats, and alligators. But it was better than the inside of a war prison. All the next day I lay in a blackberry patch, fearing to move, but feasting on the luscious, ripe berries. What a contrast it was to my previous starving! Never in this world shall I enjoy food so again.

Near to me was a watering-station for the railway to Atlanta. As I lay in the bushes I heard trains halting all day. With night came a glorious moon. Such a flood of heaven's own light I had never seen before. By ten at night a long, empty train halted, and in two minutes I had sprung from the bushes and was inside of an empty freight car. In ten minutes more I stood in the door of the car watching the fair farms and the hamlets of Georgia sleeping under the glorious moonlight, while I was being hurled along heaven knew where.

That was the strangest ride of my life. The conductor came along when we were near Atlanta, swinging his lantern into the cars, and found a strange passenger. He threatened all sorts of things if my fare were not paid, of course I had no money, but I put myself on my dignity, told him I was a convalescent soldier coming back from a furlough, and dared him or any other civilian to put me off the train. That ended the colloquy, and just before daylight the whistle screamed for Atlanta, and I was inside the lines of Hood's army.

I left the train and in a few moments was tucked away in the hay-mow of a barn near the station. So far, good; but daylight brought a squad of Rebel cavalry into the barn, who, to my dismay, soon commenced climbing up to the mow for hay for their horses. My presence of mind was about leaving me utterly when I happened to notice an empty sugar hogshead in the corner of the mow. Before the Rebels were up I was in it, and there I sat and perspired for six mortal hours. Those hours were days, every one of them. All of this time Sherman's army, then besieging Atlanta, was throwing shells into our neighbourhood. At last, at last! the Rebels saddled their horses and rode out of the barnyard.

I was not long in changing my headquarters. For days and days I walked up and down Atlanta among the troops, to the troops, away from the troops, always moving, always just going to the regiment, to which I had attached myself as ordnance sergeant. I was very careful, however, to keep far away from that particular regiment. I knew its position, its chief officers, knew, in fact, the position of every brigade in Hood's army. It was to my interest, under the circumstances, to know them well, for I was continually halted with such exclamations as, "Hallo! which way? Where's your regiment? What you doing away over here?"

A hundred times I was on the point of being arrested and carried to my alleged command. For every man I met I had a different tale, to suit the circumstances. At night I slept where I could—under a tree, behind a drygoods box; it made little difference, as my lying down on the ground, hungry, pillowless, and blanketless, and fearing every moment to be arrested, could not be called sleeping. This life was growing monotonous at last; the more so as, aside from an occasional apple, I had nothing at all to eat.

About the fifth day I overheard an old Irishman, hoeing among his potatoes, bitterly reviling the war to his wife. I made his acquaintance and discovered our sentiments as to the rebellion to be very nearly identical. Under the most tremendous of oaths as to secrecy, I told who I was and that I was absolutely starving. If he would help me, I knew how to save his property when Sherman's army should enter. That it would enter, and that Atlanta would be razed to the ground, and every human being's throat cut, he had not a doubt. Still, if detected in secreting or feeding me, he would be hanged from his own door-post. There was no doubting that, either.

However, that night I slept in his cellar and was fed with more than the crumbs from his table. It was arranged that I should wander about the army daytimes, and come to his cellar—unknown to him, of course—about ten every night, when his family were likely to be in bed. The outside door was to be left unlocked for me. Prisoners did not carry timepieces in the South. Mine disappeared with my pistols on the battlefield of Chattanooga, and as an unfortunate result I went to my den in the cellar an hour too early one evening. None of my protector's family seemed to have been aware of the guest in the cellar.

I was sitting quietly in a corner of the dark, damp place when the trap-door opened above and a young lady, bearing a lamp, descended and seemed to be searching for something. It was a romantic situation—destined to be more so. Groping about the cellar, the young lady approached me. I moved along the wall to avoid her. She unluckily followed. I moved farther again. She followed, cornered me, screamed at the top of her voice, dropped the lamp, and fainted. In half a minute three soldiers who had happened to be lunching upstairs, the old lady, and my friend, her husband, rushed down the steps, armed with lights. The old gentleman recognized me and was in despair. I think I too was in despair, but, rightfully or wrongfully, I took to my heels and escaped through the door which I had entered, leaving the fainting girl, the despairing father, and the astonished soldiers to arrange matters as they might. The girl recovered, I learned years afterward, and her father's house was one of the few that escaped the flames when Sherman started to the sea.

From that night on I slept again at the roadsides, and as for rations, I might say I did not have any. The weather was terribly hot, but I spent my days wandering from regiment to regiment and from fort to fort, inspecting the positions and the works. I knew if I did get through, all this would be equal to any army corps for Sherman.

Once I crept into a little deserted frame house and, happening to find an old white palmetto hat there, I changed it for my own, on account of the heat. I then laid my Rebel jacket and cap under the boards and, fastening my pantaloons up with a piece of broad red calico that happened to be with the hat, sallied out, seeing what I could see. I very soon saw more than I had calculated on. I had wandered well off to the right of the army and was quietly looking about when a squad of cavalry dashed in, shouting, "The Yankees are on us!" There was a regiment of infantry close by, which sprang to its feet, and every man in sight was ordered to seize a gun and hurry to the front. I, too, was picked up, and before I had time to explain that I was just going over to my division a gun was in my hands and I was pushed into the line. The whole force ran for a quarter of an hour into the woods, firing as they ran, and shouting. Suddenly, as a few shots were fired into us, we stopped and formed line of battle.

The skirmish was soon over. Some cavalry had flanked the Yanks and brought them in, and while their pockets were being gone through with by my fellow-soldiers I slipped to the rear, and was glad to get back into my own cap and jacket.

I lay in the little empty house that night. Sherman's army had been banging at the city fearfully, and setting houses on fire all night. It was a little revenge, I presume, for the losses in the skirmish in which I had

71

taken so picturesque a part. These shelled houses had emptied their occupants into the street, and a little after daylight I noticed a family, with its worldly baggage piled on a one-mule wagon, stop in front of my residence. "Here's a house out of range of bullets. Why not move in?" I heard a manly voice call to the women and children, following with the traps.

"Move in," I thought to myself. "Well, they can stand it, if I can." The house consisted of but one large room, unceiled, and reaching to the rafters, with the exception of a small compartment, finished off and ceiled, in one corner. On top of this little compartment were my headquarters.

In they moved, bag and baggage, and the women folks soon commenced preparing a meal outside, under the shadows of the front door. This half-finished room had been used as a butcher shop in the past, it seemed, and the meat hooks in the corner had served me as a ladder to mount to my perch on the ceiling. "Now, Johnny," chirped the wife, "do run uptown and buy some red and white muslin. We will make a Union flag, and when Sherman gits in, as he's bound to, we're jest as good Union folks as he is. You know I'm dyin' for real coffee. I'm tired of chicory and Injun bread, and I don't keer if Sherman's folks is in tomorrow. We'll draw government rations, and be Union."

These good people were probably "poor trash" of the South, not caring much which way the war went provided they could get rations. Their general talk, however, was of the real Rebel character, and it was an unsafe place for me to stop in. In an hour the banquet before the front door was prepared, and all hands went out to partake. Soon they were joined by a Rebel soldier, who seemed to be on a half-hour's furlough to visit the young lady of the party, whom I took to be his sweetheart. Sherman's army, I was sorry to learn from this soldier, was being simply "mowed out of existence." "All the woods about Atlanta were as a reeking corpse." Sherman himself was in flight northward.

By looking more closely through a chink in the weather-boarding of my hiding-place I discovered that he was reading all this dreadful information from a Copperhead newspaper from Chicago, and then I felt easier.

Again, there was the talk about money purses made of Yankee's scalps and finger rings from Yankee bones; and during the dinner I was no little astonished to see this valiant Southerner exhibit to his eager listeners a veritable ring, rough and yellow, made, as he said, from the bones of one of Sherman's cavalrymen. This was probably brag.

The banquet of cucumbers, chicory, and Injun bread was about terminating. My soldier with the ring had used up his furlough and was gone. The house was still empty, and it was now, or never, if I proposed getting down from my perch without alarm. My plan was silently to climb down the meat hooks which I had ascended and to slip out at the still open back door of the house. On peeping over the edge of the ceiling, however, what was my amazement to see a bull-dog of immense proportions tied to one of my hooks!

Here was a "situation!" He was sound asleep, but had an amiable countenance. I dropped a bit of plaster on his nose. He looked up amazed, and smiled. Then I smiled, and then he smiled again; and then I carefully crept down, patted him on the head, said goodbye in a whisper, and in a twinkling was out at the back door. My gratitude to this dog is boundless.

I had found it unsafe to be about houses, and again I took my lodgings in the field. Again I was busy, just *going to my division*, but never getting there. Once, near the sacred quarters of a brigadier, the guard arrested me. I protested, and our loud talk brought the brigadier to the rescue. I explained how I was "just going to my regiment," and how my pass had been lost, and the necessity of my going on at once. The brigadier took in the situation at a glance, and with a pencil wrote me a pass, good for that day.

Fighting was going on about Atlanta constantly, but with so many apparent reverses to our arms that I feared I should never get away.

The memorable 22nd of July came, and with it the most terrific fighting on Hood's right, and in fact all round the semi-circle about the city. A division, with my Alabama regiment, entered the battle on Hood's right wing, and I followed, at a safe distance, as an ordnance sergeant. Everybody was too busy and excited to ask me questions, and in the hope that Hood would be defeated and an opportunity for getting through the lines be at last presented, I was feeling good. Hundreds, thousands possibly, of wounded men fell back by me, but all shouting, "The Yankees are beaten, and McPherson is killed."

It was too true! McPherson had fallen and, if reports were correct, Sherman's army had met with an awful disaster. For me, there was nothing left but to get back to the rear and try another direction. I knew that Sherman's advance was at the ford, at Sandtown, on the Chattahoochie River, at our left. Could I only get there, I might still be saved. I had now been seen among the Rebel forts and troops so much that there was the greatest danger of my being recaptured, and shot as a spy. On the night of the 22nd I took refuge under a hedge, near to a field hospital.

No food and no sleep for days was killing me. Still there was no rest, for all the night long I heard the groans of the poor fellows whose arms and legs were being chopped off by the surgeons. The whole night was simply horrible. I might have died there myself; I wonder that I did not. Only the hope of escape was keeping me alive. I had not eaten a pound of food in days.

Daylight of the 23rd came. It was my birthday. Auspicious day, I thought, and again my hopes gave me strength and courage to work my way past lines of infantry and cavalry.

All day, till nearly sunset, I had crept around in the woods, avoiding sentinels, and now I was almost in sight of the longed-for goal. It was not a mile to the ford. When darkness set in I should swim the river and be a free man. More, I had news that would help Sherman's army to capture Atlanta. A thousand pictures of home, of freedom, peace, were painting themselves in my mind. One hour more, and all would be well.

Hark! a shot, and then a call to halt and hold up my arms. I was surrounded in a moment by fifty cavalrymen who had been secreted in the bushes—how or where I know not. We were in sight of the river, and the Union flag was just beyond. It was no use here to talk about being a Confederate. I was arrested as a spy, and in great danger of being shot then and there, without a hearing. I was partly stripped, searched thoroughly, and then marched between two cavalrymen to General Ross, of Texas, who, with his staff, was also at a hidden point in the woods. General Ross treated me kindly and gave me lunch and a blanket to rest on. It was his duty, however, to send me to the division headquarters, to be tried. I was again marched till nine at night, when I was turned over to General H———. He was sitting by a fire in the woods roasting potatoes and reviling the Yankees.

As I was arrested as a spy, and to be tried, I deemed it best to say nothing. "Try to escape from me tonight," shouted General H———, as if he were commanding an army corps, "and I'll put you where there is no more 'scaping." Through the whole night a soldier sat at my head with a cocked pistol, but for the first time in days I slept soundly. Why not? The worst had happened. By daylight a guard marched me up to the city, where Hood had army headquarters in the yard of a private residence.

On the way there my guard, a mere boy, was communicative, and I persuaded him to show me the paper that was being sent around with me, from one headquarters to another. I read it. Sure enough, I was considered a spy, and was being forwarded for trial. The paper gave the hour and place of my capture, with the statement that one of those capturing me had seen me inspecting a fort on the previous Sunday.

When we reached Hood's tents, in the dooryard of the Atlanta mansion, I was turned over to a new guard, and the document brought with me was carelessly thrown into an open pigeon-hole of a desk out on the grass by a clerk who seemed too much disturbed about other matters to ask where the guard came from or what I was accused of. I, at least, noticed where the paper was put. There was the most tremendous excitement at headquarters. Orderlies and officers were dashing everywhere at once, fighting was constantly going on, and an immediate retreat seemed to be determined.

I was left that night in a tent with a few other prisoners, among them two deserters, sentenced to be shot. Close by on the lawn was the desk where the clerk had deposited my paper. Our guard was very accommodating, or very negligent, for he allowed different persons to go in and out from our tent at all hours during the night. Daylight brought the provost-marshal general to the tent, to dispose of the prisoners. The name of each was called, and all but myself were taken out, heard, and sent off.

"And who are you?" he said, pleasantly enough to me. I stepped forward. The clerk was asked for the paper, but it was gone. "It certainly had been misplaced," said the clerk, in embarrassment. He had put it in that particular pigeon-hole. I testified to that myself, and added,—this sudden inspiration coming to me in the emergency,— that "it was of little consequence, as it was from an officer,—I didn't know whom,—who had simply picked me up as an escaped prisoner." The provost-marshal took me aside and asked me if I had been about the works or the troops any. I told him my name, that I was really an escaped prisoner, and that I had just walked up from Macon and had hoped to get away. "You have had a hard time of it," he said, "and I almost wish you had got away. I hope you will soon be free," he added, "and that the cruel war is almost over." It was a sudden and great relief to me to know that now I was not to be regarded as a spy. What became of the "papers" and the charges against me afterward in the midst of war excitements, I never knew. The next night the provost-marshal sent me under guard back to Macon prison whence I had escaped.

CHAPTER 12

Under Fire of Our Own Guns at Charleston

I was scarcely returned to the Macon prison again when two hundred of us, all officers, were selected to be placed under the fire from our navy then bombarding Charleston. By some wonderful fiction of military law the "Confederates," as the Rebels called themselves, pretended to regard the bombardment of Charleston as a crime. I do not remember now how the selection of victims to be sent to Charleston was made one evening about the end of July, 1864. This, however, happened that night, to add adventure and excitement to the Charleston trip. The greater number of those selected were members of a "Secret Band" of prisoners who had resolved to mutiny or to do any act in our power that could result in our escape from captivity. I recall how Major Marshall one afternoon secretly administered to me the oath of this desperate band.

With my hand on my heart I swore to instantly obey every order given to me by the "head captain." I was to ask no questions, but to strike, whenever told; to kill, no matter whom, even were my own brother to be the victim. I was ready to do anything. I had been mistreated and starved long enough. Death could be little worse than all of us had been undergoing for months. The news coming to us from our prison comrades at Andersonville was perfectly horrible. History had never related the like of it. We received the *Telegraph*, a Macon newspaper, into the prison pen every morning. At the head of one of its columns each day the editor reported the awful number of poor starving creatures who had died at Andersonville the day before. It was not unlike the reports of the number of dumb beasts killed each day in the Chicago slaughter pens. Pretty soon I learned that the eighty comrades of my regiment captured with me at Missionary Ridge were nearly every one dead. The details of their sufferings were too horrible to dilate upon. We wondered sometimes if God had forsaken the world.

We who joined the "Band," and took the awful oath we did, knew what it all meant. Outside our stockade loaded cannon waited but the least alarm to fire upon us. On top of the stockade guards walked day and night with orders to instantly kill any prisoner who should approach within twelve feet of the high wall. We were only eight hundred prisoners all told, and nothing to fight with but naked hands. Outside whole regiments armed to the teeth lay with guns in their hands waiting to destroy every one of us should we offer to escape. What was our chance? Almost nothing; or if anything, death! Still we resolved to try.

Then came that night when we were to get on the cars and start for Charleston. Instantly the word was passed along for every member of the secret "Band" to quietly arm himself with a short club, made from our bunks and sheds, and to keep it hid under his coat or blanket. Now we were counted and put into a train of box cattle cars. Twenty-five prisoners were in a car, and in the side door of each car stood a guard with his loaded musket. We who were not leaders of the "Band" wondered what desperate thing we were about to try. I do not know where the tools came from, but when the train was well in motion, and the noise deadened our movements, a big hole, large enough to permit a man to creep through, was knocked in the end of each car. The darkness, the crowd in the cars and the noise prevented the guards knowing what was going on. This was the first *"vestibule"* railroad train ever made.

Shortly now one of our leaders came creeping along from car to car, and in a low voice he told us what was about to happen. The train on its way to Charleston would halt close to the sea at a little town called Pocotaligo. We knew that some ships of the Union navy lay out in the water there, scarce a dozen miles away. The design was to seize on our guards as we reached the village, disarm them, kill them, if necessary, ditch the train, destroy the road and the telegraph, and then escape to the ships. I think not a soul of us doubted the likelihood of our success. We would be free men on the morrow if all went well. It would be two or three o'clock in the night when the train would pass the point of action. Every one of us had his club and his pocket knife in his hand ready to strike.

At the proper moment Colonel ——, our leader, with three comrades, was to spring through the end of the front car where he was, onto the tender, seize the engineer and fireman and wave a lantern violently as a signal for us to suddenly lay hold of every Rebel soldier on the train. Ten miles out from Pocotaligo our hearts beat in terrible excitement. No one spoke; we only waited. It was silence, all save the rumbling of the car wheels.

So far our guards seemed in perfect ignorance of the approaching danger. Five miles out, so sure were we of success, a few began to act without waiting for the signal. In one or two of the cars the guards had been suddenly seized and their muskets were in our hands. In the car where I was, one of the astonished guards, finding himself without a gun, coolly said: "And what are you 'uns going to do with we 'uns?" It was a tremendous moment, as the train sped along in the dark. Three miles to Pocotaligo; two miles; one mile. With quick beating heart I leaned from our car door, straining my eyes for the lantern signal. Then the whistle blew loudly, but the train only hastened its speed, and in two minutes, instead of stopping, we shot past the station at lightning speed.

What had happened? Were we discovered? Not a signal had been given to us. In the morning we were all hurried inside the jail yard of Charleston. Now we knew it all. At the crucial moment our leader *had lost his nerve* and *become a coward*; or had he betrayed us? He had not waved the lantern, though he had captured it, and held it in his hand. We were now much alarmed as to what would be done with us for seizing the guards. We might lose our lives. Colonel ——, the false leader, was taken to another prison to save him from being torn to pieces by his own comrades.

The newspapers of Charleston that morning contained flaming articles, describing how a terrible catastrophe had been averted by the cowardice or treason of one man. Where they got the details of the proposed capture of the train, no one will ever know. Was the leader simply a coward, or was he paid for betraying us?

After a while we were transferred to what was called the "Roper Hospital." It was close to the jail, and the danger of being killed by the shells from our own fleet was still very great, though, in fact, few of us were hurt. The yellow fever was to be a greater scourge than Yankee cannon.

Our fleet officers had learned the locality where the prisoners were guarded, and fired their shells mostly in other directions. It was a grand spectacle at night—the soaring through the heavens of so many blazing bombshells and their bursting in the city. Parts of Charleston that we could see were perfect pictures of desolation; whole quarters stood in black ruins and uninhabited. The weather was exceedingly hot, and the yellow fever broke out and raged fearfully among both prisoners and guards. It seemed as if we should all die there. At last they transported us away to a little open field in the woods, close to the town of Columbia, the capital of South Carolina.

The surgeon of the prison camp at Charleston was Dr. Todd, a brother of President Lincoln's wife. A more rabid Secessionist was nowhere to be found. It was a curious situation, that the brother-in-law of the great President should be so attached to the country's opponents.

On our way to the prison at Columbia Major Marshall of my regiment and two captains escaped from the train and reached the North by tramping at night through the mountains of North Carolina and Tennessee. They had horrible experiences for many weeks.

CHAPTER 13

Living in a Grave

Now we were near the capital of South Carolina. It is our third prison. We were placed in a cleared field among the pine woods, a few miles from the town. Here we spent a part of a terrible winter exposed to the storm and rain. We had no shelter save such as we made at last of sticks and logs that we were allowed to carry in from the neighbouring wood. Our food was wretched, we had almost no clothing, and the weather was very bad nearly all the time. We were surrounded by a line of guards. A battery constantly in readiness to fire on us should an alarm be given stood nearby. Our food was still the half-cooked corn and cobs together, with quantities of a poor and sickly sorghum molasses. We heard that the Rebel army was living little better than we were. In ridicule of the rations the prisoners dubbed this prison pen "Camp Sorghum."

Every man among us was sick with diarrheal. The little graveyard for the prisoners nearby grew rapidly. The details of our life in this miserable camp I shall not relate. They were simply too horrible. As for myself,—my only shelter was a hole in the ground, four feet deep, four feet wide and eight feet long. It was covered with boughs and earth. Lieutenant Morris and myself occupied this living grave for months. We had a tiny fire-place of clay built in the end of it, where we burned roots, and the long rainy nights we two sat there alone, reading an old newspaper by our root-light or talking of our far-away homes. One very stormy night our water-soaked roof fell in on us, and then we were compelled to walk about in the rain. I wonder now that any soul survived the miseries of that camp. Valley Forge was paradise compared to it. But all this misery was a part of war.

Naturally, numbers ran the guard lines at this woeful prison pen and escaped into the woods. Firing by the sentinels on these escaping prisoners was a common occurrence on dark nights. Here and there an officer was killed, and sometimes under circumstances that marked the sentinel a common murderer. A battery of loaded cannons stood outside the guard line, with orders to open on the prisoners should five musket shots be heard. With the constant escaping of prisoners at night these five fatal shots could occur at any hour.

For my own part, I resolved to again attempt escape, but my efforts failed again, and twice in succession. I recall with a shudder how one night late in November my friend, Lieutenant Ecking of New York, was foully murdered. He had bribed a guard to let two or three of us run across the line that night at midnight. The bribe was to consist of a silver watch. Some of these men were easily bribed. They were not regular Confederate soldiers, but usually cowardly home guards, who regarded the murdering of a helpless prisoner a heroic act.

When midnight came three of us were secreted close to the dead line. As soon as the bribed sentinel came to his post and commenced walking up and down his beat Lieutenant Ecking rose and approached him. The night was clear moonlight. The moment Ecking had crossed the dead line, and was holding the watch up to the guard, the coward shot him dead. For this outrage the home guard received a furlough.

About this time, too, Lieutenant Turbayne was murdered by a guard for mistaking the ringing of a bell. Some of us had been permitted to go out on parole and carry in wood at stated times. Without notice, this privilege was suspended, but the bellman, by mistake, rang as usual. Turbayne started for the dead line. "Go back, halt!" shouted a sentinel. Turbayne turned to obey, but was instantly shot in the back and dropped dead. There was a furious commotion among the prisoners. The guards, too, collected about the spot. The Rebel officer in charge left his lunch and walked over also. He held in his hand a great piece of pumpkin pie, and continued eating from it as he stood there by the corpse of the man they had murdered. There was almost a mutiny in the prison camp, and one proper leader at that moment would have put an end to the whole Rebel outfit. In the end it would have been death to the whole of us.

Previous to this threatened outbreak I had again tried my own chance at escaping. It was now November 4, 1864, a cold blustering day, and the prisoners in their rags and almost barefooted stood and shivered in the naked field. At four o'clock a dozen were paroled and allowed to go out to the woods and carry in some fuel.

Lieutenant Fritchie and myself managed to mix ourselves among this little paroled company, and forgot to return to the enclosure. We helped a little in the fuel getting, and then suddenly disappeared in the pine forests. For some days we crept about in the great pine woods, scarcely knowing our direction or where we were going. Our leaving had been so sudden that we were planless. Here and there we stumbled onto a darkey, who never hesitated to bring us corn hoe cake or whatever eatables he might happen to have in his cabin. The slaves universally were the prisoners' friends, and they knew a hundred times more about the war and its object than their plantation masters ever supposed. Many an escaping prisoner was fed by them and, with the north star as a guide, conducted to safety. Many an army movement was made possible by loyal negroes. Barring an occasional Union white man, they were the only friends the soldiers had in the South.

Lieutenant Fritchie and I had some queer adventures while we wandered about the woods of South Carolina during this little leave of absence from the Confederates. We did not see a single white man, save one, and he tried to shoot us. One night we lodged in an open-topped corn-crib, not knowing in the darkness that we were quite close to an inhabited farmhouse. When daylight came we peeped over the corn-crib and were much astonished to see a woman at her wash-tub on the back porch of a cabin close by. She must have seen our heads, for that very moment she stopped her washing and entered the cabin. Shortly she appeared again, followed by a man, who took one long steady look at the corn-crib; then he entered the cabin, and we knew it was to get his gun. Very quick resolution and action on our part became advisable. A little ploughed field only separated our corn-crib, at the back, from a thick piece of woods. In a moment the man was out again on the porch, bearing a musket.

"Drop to the ground behind the crib and run to the woods," said Fritchie. "I'll keep watch on the man. I'll drop down too. When you are across wave your hand if he is not coming, and then I'll run." In a moment's time I was running across the ploughed field, keeping the crib between me and the porch of the cabin. The man with the musket never saw me. I waved to Fritchie; he, too, started on the run, and to this hour I laugh to myself when I picture to my mind Fritchie, a short, stumpy fellow, tumbling absolutely heels over head in his haste to cover that bit of ploughed ground.

Very shortly we heard bloodhounds bellowing. We knew too well what that meant. Numbers of escaping prisoners had been torn to pieces by them. That was the common way of catching runaway slaves and prisoners of war down South. They hunt "niggers" that way today down there, (as at time of first publication).

By hard running, turns and counter-turns, and frequent crossing and recrossing little streams, we threw the dogs off our track, and slept until night in the thicket. The wind blew hard and cold that night, and as we stood secreted under a thorn-tree by the roadside two men passed, so close we could have touched them. Something told us they, too, were escaping prisoners. We tried to attract their attention enough to be sure. One of us spoke, scarcely more than whisper. Instantly and in alarm the two men bounded away like scared wolves. Days afterward we found out that they had been not only fleeing prisoners, but were, indeed, two of our personal friends.

The next night was fair, and a full round moon lighted up the sandy desert with its oasis of tall, immense pine trees. The white winding road of sand that seemed to have been abandoned for a hundred years was almost trackless. Here and there, too, we saw an abandoned turpentine camp, the spiles still in the trees and the troughs lying rotting at their feet.

There was nothing but silence there, and loneliness, and moonlight. Here in the quiet night, if anywhere in the world, two poor escaping prisoners of war would be in no danger of a foe.

For hours we trudged along, going where we knew not, when suddenly to our amazement two mounted cavalrymen stood right in our way and called to us to surrender. There was nothing to do but to obey. Our capture had been an accident. These two officers, a captain and a lieutenant, had been riding the country trying to catch some deserters from their army and had blundered on to us. They started with us to Lexington jail, some miles away. The captain rode a dozen yards or so ahead, with a revolver in his hand. I trudged along in the sand at his side, faithfully hanging on to his stirrup strap. The lieutenant and Fritchie followed us in a like manner in the moonlight.

It seems to have been a romantic occasion, when I think of it now; we two Federals and these two Confederates, there alone in the moonlight, and the big pine trees and the white sands about. I could not help reflecting, though, how many a captured prisoner had never been accounted for. Possibly we should never see Lexington jail. It would be an easy thing for these men to leave our bodies there in the sand somewhere. There were few words at first as we plodded our slow way in the moonlight. At last my captain and I entered into lively conversation about the South in general, and then both of us hoped the war would soon come to an end. To my surprise the young captain confided to me that he was, at heart, a Union man. "And why in the Confederate army?" I asked, in astonishment. "Because," said the captain, "everybody in my village in South Carolina is. I would have been hooted to death had I remained at home. My father is a rich man; he is opposed to the war, but he, too, is in the service at Richmond."

"Under the circumstances," I said, "I being Union, and you being Union, why not look the other way a moment and let me try the time required to reach yonder clump of trees." "No, not a thought of it," he answered almost hotly. "You are my prisoner, I will do my duty." The subject was dropped, and in half an hour Fritchie and I were inside a stone cell in Lexington jail. "You can lie down on the stone floor and sleep if you want to," the jailer said, crustily. The two young officers said a cheery goodbye and went away.

Before daybreak the door of our cell opened again and the gruff jailer called, "Which of you is Adjutant Byers." Then he pushed a basket and blanket in to me, and a little note. The basket was full of good warm food and the little note, in a woman's hand, said: "With the compliments of the captain's wife."

I think tears came to the eyes of both of us there in that cell that night. It was among the few kindnesses I ever experienced in the Confederacy. Of course it was a woman's act. The captain had gone to his home nearby and told his wife about his prisoners, and here was the remembrance. The world is not so bad after all, we said to each other, Fritchie and I.

The next day the jailer paraded us out in the corridor, and I think all the people in the county came to see us, to remark on us, and touch us with their hands. Most of these men, women, and children had absolutely never seen a Northern man before, and a Yankee soldier was a greater curiosity than a whole menagerie of polar bears. I saw the ignorance of the "poor white trash" of the South that day. Not one in twenty of them knew what the war was about. The negroes had a more intelligent notion of affairs than did the people of the Carolinas.

In a few days Fritchie and I were conducted back to our prison pen near Columbia, South Carolina.

Shortly they moved us once more. This time to the high-walled yard of the lunatic asylum, inside the city. As they marched us through the streets we could see how beautiful the little capital of South Carolina was. It had handsome shops and residences, and beautiful shade trees everywhere gave it a most attractive appearance. It was almost the best known city of the South and here the fatal heresy of secession had been born. As we went along the streets a mob of people gathered around us, hooting and hissing their hatred at us, just as they had done that first time we were taken through the town. A few wanted the guards to give them a chance to hang us. It was a sorry sight—this band of ragged, helpless, hungry loyalists being led like slaves and animals through the hooting, threatening crowd. That mob, thirsting for our blood, did not dream what was about to happen.

Here now in Columbia we were walled in just as we had been at Macon, and our lives continued in much the same hardship as before. Only here I do not recall that any prisoner was murdered. It is right to say, too, that the outrages so often committed on prisoners here and elsewhere in the South were not by the regular Confederate soldiers, but by home guards usually set over us. It seems now, when I recall it, that life was not quite so bad here. We soon had some boards given us; so we built sheds to live in. As for myself, I, with three or four comrades, lived in a little wedge tent. It was very cold and midwinter now. I scarcely slept at night, but walked about to keep warm. It was on one of these midnight tramps that it occurred to me to write the song, "Sherman's March to the Sea." I recur to it here because it gave its name to the great campaign it celebrates.

The story of how it came to be written cannot perhaps be wholly without interest. During the days that Sherman's army was tramping from Atlanta toward Savannah we prisoners were not permitted to have any news from the outside of any kind whatever. There was a fear that if we knew what was going on a mutiny might follow. We were constantly being told by our guards that Sherman's invading army was being headed off or destroyed. In the beginning we feared these stories to be true, but the uneasy actions and sullen looks of our captors soon began to belie their statements. As said, three or four of us prisoners occupied a little wedge tent. A negro had recently been allowed to come into the prison pen mornings to sell bread to those who had any money with which to buy.

Our little mess got a small loaf now every morning; not more for the bread, though we needed that badly enough, than for a certain little roll of paper carefully hidden away in the middle of the loaf. It was a Columbia morning newspaper printed on soft thin paper and of extremely small size. Our loyal negro had easily enough been persuaded to hide a copy of this paper in the bread for us as often as he could have the chance unobserved. A knowing wink from him told us when to eat our loaf of bread inside the tent and with one of us watching at the door while another read in a low voice the news from the invading army. The paper rolled up was not larger than a walnut.

It was full of misrepresentations and reports of disasters to Sherman, to mislead the Georgians and lessen their alarm. Yet between the lines we easily enough read that Sherman was surely marching on, and victorious. His columns were coming nearer to us; and how we longed night and day that he might capture the prison! At last we saw that there was no hope. He was passing us,—though, but many miles away.

Then one morning, when we unrolled the little paper in the bread and read it, we knew that *he had reached the sea.* Savannah had fallen. The consternation of the Southerners was tremendous. But, next, they pretended that they could box Sherman up in Savannah and capture his whole army.

One December night when I was tramping up and down the prison pen in the dark, trying to keep warm, I reflected on the tremendous importance of what Sherman had done. And I wondered what so curious a campaign would be called. It was not a series of battles—it was a great *march.* And then the title, and almost the words, of the song came to me.

The next morning when my tent comrades were out of doors shivering over a little fire I remained in our little heap of straw, and completed the verses.

I went out to the fire and read them to my comrades. A Lieutenant Rockwell happened to be present and asked permission to make a copy of the verses. He, with many others, slept on the ground under the hospital building. One had to crawl on his hands and knees to enter there. There was a most capable Glee Club among the officers, and they had by some means secured a flute, violins, and bass viol for accompaniments. They kept their instruments under the house, too, where they slept.

Every afternoon this Glee Club was permitted to sing and play on the little elevated porch of the hospital. The only condition was that Southern songs should be sung, not less than Northern songs. There was no trouble about that. The songs of our captors were better than no songs. Besides, these singers made music. All the crowd of prisoners, eight hundred now, often stood in front of the little porch to enjoy the singing. Almost hundreds of the Rebels, too, together with many ladies of Columbia, climbed up onto the walls, where the guards stood, and applauded the singers as much as any.

One drizzly afternoon I was standing by a little persimmon tree in the midst of the crowd listening to the songs, when Major Isett, leader of the Glee Club, said: "Now we will have a song about Sherman." To my astonishment, it was my "Sherman's March to the Sea."

It was received in a tremendous fashion. Everybody cheered and hurrahed. The news of Sherman's victories was fresh upon them. In five minutes' time the good fortune of my song was settled. The name of the author was loudly called for; someone saw me by the little tree, and I was quickly hauled to the front and up onto the platform. In a few moments an unknown officer among the many prisoners became a sort of prison hero.

Everybody wanted the song, everybody sang it; and clever penmen made a good thing making copies at twenty dollars apiece, Confederate money. As a little compliment to me the captain of the prison allowed me to sleep on the floor of the hospital room. To me that was important, as shall appear. Later in this narrative, too, will be seen how an exchanged prisoner, by the name of Tower, who had an artificial leg, carried the song in this wooden limb through the lines to our soldiers in the North, where it was sung everywhere and with demonstration. In a week it had given its name to the campaign, and a million copies of it soon passed into circulation.

Lieutenant Rockwell, who had asked my leave to copy the verses that first morning, was a composer, and there in the dust under the old hospital he had, unknown to me, written the first music to which the song was ever sung. Later, it had many other settings, but that one, though difficult, remained the best. The song has often since been sung to the air of "The Red, White, and Blue." This is the history of the song, which I print here as a part of this narrative.

SHERMAN'S MARCH TO THE SEA

Our camp fires shone bright on the mountains
That frowned on the river below,
While we stood by our guns in the morning
And eagerly watched for the foe—
When a rider came out from the darkness
That hung over mountain and tree,
And shouted, "Boys, up and be ready,
For Sherman will march to the sea."

Then cheer upon cheer for bold Sherman
Went up from each valley and glen,
And the bugles re-echoed the music
That came from the lips of the men.
For we knew that the stars in our banner
More bright in their splendour would be,
And that blessings from Northland would greet us
When Sherman marched down to the sea.

Then forward, boys, forward to battle,
We marched on our wearisome way,
And we stormed the wild hills of Resaca,—
God bless those who fell on that day—
Then Kenesaw, dark in its glory,
Frowned down on the flag of the free,
But the East and the West bore our standards,
And Sherman marched on to the sea.

Still onward we pressed, till our banners
Swept out from Atlanta's grim walls,
And the blood of the patriot dampened
The soil where the traitor flag falls;
But we paused not to weep for the fallen,
Who slept by each river and tree;
Yet we twined them a wreath of the laurel
As Sherman marched down to the sea.

O, proud was our army that morning
That stood where the pine darkly towers,
When Sherman said: "Boys, you are weary,
This day fair Savannah is ours."
Then sang we a song for our chieftain
That echoed over river and lea,
And the stars in our banner shown brighter
When Sherman marched down to the sea.

[*Sherman's March to the Sea.*—From *Eggleston's Famous War Ballads.*—

General Sherman, in a recent conversation with the editor of this collection, declared that it was this poem with its phrase, "*march to the sea,*" that threw a glamour of romance over the campaign which it celebrates. Said General Sherman:

The thing was nothing more or less than a change of base; an operation perfectly familiar to every military man, but a poet got hold of it, gave it the captivating label, 'The March to the Sea,' and the unmilitary public made a romance out of it.

It may be remarked that the general's modesty overlooks the important fact that the romance lay really in his own deed of derring-do; the poet merely recorded it, or at most interpreted it to the popular intelligence. The glory of the great campaign was Sherman's and his army's; the joy of celebrating it was the poet's; the admiring memory of it is the people's.—Original Editor.]

As stated, I slept nights now on the floor of the prison hospital. This added comfort, however, did not tempt me to stay in prison, if I could get away. Once more we heard that the prisoners were to be carted away to some safer place, out of the line of Sherman's army, now turned North and moving rapidly toward us. A night or two before this move of prisoners really commenced Lieutenant Devine of Philadelphia joined me in an effort to get away. The walls of the least used room of the hospital were made of joined boards. By the use of an old case knife, hacked into a saw, or auger, we managed to cut a hole sufficiently large to permit us to pull ourselves through and out into an attic above a little porch. We repaired the boards as best we could and crept out into the dark hole.

It was the attic of the same porch on which our Glee Club stood when they sang my song. It was a little cramped up place we were in, where we could neither sit erect nor lie at full length. There were no guards inside the prison hospital; the night was very dark; the sick prisoners seemed to be sleeping. A dim lamp hung from the ceiling. We were not detected. The next night at midnight, when the prisoners were being marched away, two of them were missing. What a night and day and part of another night that was for us, crooked and cramped as we were, in the top of that little porch.

At the next midnight, when every soul, prisoners, guards and all, seemed to be gone far away and dead silence was upon the place, Devine and I crept down from our hiding place. The big gate was closed and locked. By the aid of a scantling I managed to get up onto the high brick wall.

My surprise was immense to see guards waiting for us outside, and to know that we were discovered. One of the guards rushed up to his post at the top of the wall, but he was too late to shoot; we were already in hiding among the empty board huts and barracks.[1]

In a moment the big gate opened and a hundred men rushed in, looking for the escaping Yankees. They howled, they cursed at us, they set the barracks on fire. Then amid the *mêlée* and excitement in the dark my comrade and myself pulled our gray blankets about us, picked up a water bucket each, and pushed up to the guard at the gate. We were "going for water," we said. "The lieutenant says the fire must be put out." Without waiting a reply we hurried out in the darkness. There were some vain shots after us.

Shortly we heard the tramp of horses coming toward us. A friendly culvert in the road into which we dodged afforded us protection while a whole company of Johnny Rebs rode over our heads. What would they have thought, that night, had they known it as they went skipping along with arms and jingling sabres, to confront Sherman's advance guards?

We were gone. After a while, in the outskirts of the city, we saw a light in a cabin and a negro walking up and down by the window. Every negro we knew to be a loyal friend. This one we called out among some rose bushes in the dooryard. Instantly, and without fear, we told him who we were and that we were in his power. There is not a question but he would have been well rewarded had he betrayed us to the Confederate soldiers in the city that night. Few words were spoken. That morning two escaped prisoners were secreted under some bean stalks in the garret of the negro's cabin. The negro's sick wife lay in the single room below. Had we been discovered now that negro would have been hanged from his own door lintel. And well he knew it.

Sherman's army was already pounding at the gates of the town. He was crossing the river and his shells reached to the capital. This much we knew from what we could hear in the yard below, for the negro's cabin stood at the edge of a green lawn where General Chestnut had his headquarters. We broke a little hole through the siding of the house, and now could see what the general and his staff were doing. We also could hear much that was said. Once we thought ourselves discovered, for we observed two or three of the general's negro servants standing in a group on the grass looking steadily toward the spot

---

1. When springing down from the top of that wall I lost my shoes—I had had them in my hand. I also let fall from my pocket the pages of this diary. I could not think of losing them, and at the risk of my life I slipped over the dead line and from under the guard's very feet, I snatched them up and ran behind one of the huts.

where our little improvised window was. What on earth were they looking at?

It was not much the old negro could give us to eat. A little dried beef and some cold corn bread; that was all, save that once he brought us a gallon of buttermilk. He had no cow, but he would not tell us where this, to us, heavenly nectar had come from.

There was much hurrying of officers back and forth at General Chestnut's headquarters, and plainly we could see there was great excitement. Our own negro was kept going back and forth into the town to pick up for us whatever news he could of the fight going on at the river. After awhile the cannonading grew louder, and it seemed to us the conflict must be right at the outskirts of the town. Then we saw General Chestnut hurriedly ride on to the headquarters' lawn, and we distinctly heard him say to an officer, "Sherman has got a bridge down. The game's up. We must evacuate." In a few minutes the sound of the guns increased, and then we saw General Chestnut call his slaves to him to bid them farewell. It was a touching scene, amid the dramatic surroundings. He seemed very kind, and some of them in their ignorance wept. "You will be free," he said. "Be good."

I thought, he too was affected as he mounted his horse and, followed by his staff, rode away. He was hardly out of sight when our negro protector came running toward the cabin. He was tremendously excited. A tall, old cylinder hat he had picked up on the way was on his head, his eyes bulged out, his hands waved like windmills; he was celebrating. In a moment the black face and the cylinder hat shot up the ladder and through the hatch-way to where we were.

"God Almighty be thanked!" he cried in a loud voice. "Massa, the Stars and Stripes are waving above the capital of South Carolina. Praise to the God Almighty!"

Sure enough, Union troops, had entered, and a flag from my own State had been run up on the State House. Instantly we bade him hurry and bring some Union soldiers to us. In his absence Devine and I stood shaking each other's hands and thanking God for our deliverance. No slave who had his chains knocked off that day by the coming of the Union army felt more thankful than we, freed from the wretchedness and horrors of fifteen months of imprisonment. Now we could see the Confederate cavalry evacuating the town. Whole companies passed, each trooper having a sheaf of oats slung to his saddle bow. Shortly our black friend returned, and with him two Union soldiers. "It is time to drink, boys," they cried out, as they fairly forced us to partake of the whisky in their canteens. When we all went down into the yard I was sure we would be recaptured, for the Rebel rear-guard was passing close to our cabin. The flying troops, however, had fish of their own to fry, and were in too much haste to be looking after us. Now, too, we were surrounded by General Chestnut's black servants, who were hopping about, giving thanks for their freedom. I asked one of them what it was they had been looking at so attentively the day before, when I had seen them gazing right at our hiding-place.

"Ha ha! massa! we just knowed you was up there all the time. Reckon you didn't like that ar buttermilk what we'uns sent you." Our negro friend then had made confidents of them, and we had been fed, without knowing it, on some of the good things from General Chestnut's kitchen. Should the general ever read this little book, I hope he will cease wondering what became of his buttermilk that day at Columbia.

Now, our two soldiers escorted us to a street where some of the army had halted and stacked arms. A Union flag hung over a stack of muskets, and no human being will ever know with what thankful heart-beatings and tears we gathered its silken folds into our arms. Now we knew that we were free. The terrible days were indeed over, and God's rainbow illumined our sky.

In half an hour the victorious veterans of Sherman's army, their great leader riding before, with bands playing and banners flying, entered the captured city. My comrade and I stood on a high door-step and saw them pass. Someone pointed us out to Sherman, and for a moment the whole moving army was halted till he greeted the freed prisoners. We two comrades lived a month in that short seventeenth day of February, 1865, in Columbia. I think we shook hands with a thousand soldiers, even with many soldiers we had never seen before. It seemed to us that everybody must be as glad to see us as we were to see them.

That night Columbia was burned to the ground amid untold horrors. The conflagration had commenced from bales of cotton that the enemy had fired and left in the street to prevent falling into the Union hands. A big wind rose toward evening and the burning cotton flakes were flying all over the city. It was a terrible spectacle that night. My comrade and I walked about the streets till nearly morning. Whole squares and streets were crumbling to ashes and tall buildings tumbled down everywhere. Here and there, too, there was a terrific explosion. It was Moscow done over on a smaller scale.

A division of Union troops, under Hazen, was sent into the town to fight the flames and to arrest every man discovered firing houses or walking around without a pass. So it happened that my comrade and myself, though but innocent spectators, were at midnight arrested and taken to provost headquarters. We very soon explained ourselves and were released and sent to comfortable quarters, where we slept till late the next day. It was four nights since we had had any sleep at all.

But the sights of that awful night will never fade from my memory. Most of the citizens of Columbia had sons or relations in the Rebel army. Half of them were dead, the army itself was flying everywhere, and in the blackness of this terrible night their fortunes were all lost, their homes were all burning up. Many wandered about wringing their hands and crying; some sat stolid and speechless in the street watching everything that they had go to destruction. A few wandered around, wholly demented.

Some of the invading soldiers tried earnestly to extinguish the flames; others broke into houses and added to the conflagration. Numbers of the Federal prisoners, who only a few weeks before had been marched through the streets like felons, had escaped, and what average human nature led them to do never will be known. There were fearful things going on everywhere. It was reported that an explosion occurred in one house and that twenty-four soldiers, carousing there, were lost in the ruins. Most of the people of Columbia would have been willing to have died that night, then and there. What had they left to live for? *This, too, was war.*

When the army entered in the afternoon, Lieutenant Devine and I, as related, stood on the high steps of a mansion and watched it pass. Shortly after a very charming young woman, a Mrs. C——, seeing us, came down and invited us into her father's house and gave us food. It was the first real food we had had for many, many months. The lady's father was a rich jeweller, and, though a Southerner, was a Union man. Her own husband, however, was somewhere in the Southern army. My comrade and I spent an entertaining hour in the mansion, and then went and walked about the city.

At six o'clock the awful cry, "The town is burning up, the town is burning up!" was heard everywhere. Devine and I at once thought of Mrs. C——and our friends of the afternoon, and hurried to their home to offer help. The flames were already across the street from there. Mrs. C——'s father was weeping in the drawing-room. Once he took me by the arm and led me to where we could see his own business establishment burning to the ground. "There goes the savings of a life," said he, in bitterness. "There is what the curse of secession has done for us; there is what Wade Hampton and the other political firebrands have done for South Carolina."

My comrade and I at once began carrying some of the more valuable goods out of the house for them, doing everything possible to help them save some remnant from their beautiful and luxurious home. We ran up and down the mansion stairs until we were almost dead with exhaustion. Everything we could save we piled into a phaeton that stood by the yard. Once the lady cried that her child was still in the house, burning up. Her shrieks pierced even the noise of that fearful night. Her alarm was without cause, for I soon found the child safe in the arms of a faithful slave nurse. She had simply carried it out of danger.

When the walls of the house seemed about to fall, Devine and I took the loaded buggy, he pulling in the shafts, I pushing behind, and, followed by the weeping family on foot, we drew it for a mile or more to the outer edge of the town. Here we left them in safety by a little wood, yet not knowing if we would ever see them again. Many of our soldiers were burnt up that night.

The next day Sherman's army left the ruins of the city behind them and marched away. They had, however, left supplies of rations for their unfortunate enemies. A train of empty wagons was also furnished for those fugitives who wished to follow the army and work their way North. Hundreds, possibly thousands, left the smoking ruins of their homes and travelled along with us in every conceivable conveyance that was heard of. Black and white, slave and free, rich and poor, joined in the procession behind the army. Mrs. C—— and her father's family were among them.

I now tried to find my regiment. It was gone. Many battles and many marches had so decimated it that the little fragment left had been disbanded and transferred into a regiment of cavalry.

Colonel Silsby, of the Tenth Iowa, offered me a place with his mess. I accepted. The colonel, as it happened, had charge of perhaps a hundred prisoners, captured on the march. Naturally, I was interested to go among them. I soon saw how much better they fared than I had done when in Southern hands. Two or three of them, as it happened, had been among the guards who had treated us so badly while we were in the prison known as "Camp Sorghum," outside of Columbia. They were perfectly terrified when they learned that I had been there under their charge. They seemed to fear instant and awful retaliation; but I thought of nothing of the kind. I was too glad just to be free to be thinking of any vengeance.

A curious incident now happened. This was the discovery, among these prisoners, of the husband of the young Mrs. C—— who had given us food in Columbia and whose belongings I and my comrade had tried to save. He was overjoyed to learn from me that his wife and child were at least alive. I instantly went to General Logan, and related to him how this man's family had been kind to me the day that I escaped. I had no trouble in securing his release. It was at Logan's headquarters, too, that I had secured money and an order for provisions to give to Edward Edwards, the black man who had been the means of my final rescue. His sick wife had kept him behind, else he would have followed the army. We left him in Columbia. Years later, as a sign of my gratitude toward this slave, I dedicated a little volume to him, in which I had described my prison life.

CHAPTER 14

The Army in the Carolinas

It was on this march in the Carolinas that General Sherman sent for me to come to army headquarters. We were two days away from Columbia. I was ashamed to go in my prison rags, so I waited. The next day the request was repeated, and Major Nichols of the staff came and said, "But you must go, it is an order." And I went. The general was sitting by a little rail fire in front of his tent, reading a newspaper, when we approached his bivouac in the woods. I was introduced. He at once told me how pleased he had been with my song, that I had written in prison about his army. Devine had given him a copy at that time when he halted his column to greet us by the door-step at Columbia. "Our boys shall all sing this song," he said; "and as for you, I shall give you a position on my staff. Tomorrow you will be furnished a horse and all that you need; and you must mess with me."

It would be very hard to express my feelings at this sudden transition from a prisoner in rags to a post at the headquarters of the great commander. I was almost overcome, but General Sherman's extreme kindness of manner and speech at last put me partly at my ease. Shortly a big coloured man, in a green coat, announced dinner. "Come," said the general, pushing me ahead of him into a tent, where a number of handsomely uniformed staff officers stood around a table waiting his approach. I was still in my rags. I could not help noticing the curious glances of the fine gentlemen, who doubtless were wondering what General Sherman had picked up now.

My embarrassment was extreme. The commander however soon told them who I was, gave me the seat at his right hand, and almost his entire conversation at the table was directed to me. The officers of the staff quickly took the general's cue, and I was soon an object of interest, even to them.

He directed a hundred questions to me as to the general treatment of war prisoners in the South, and he, as well as the staff, interested themselves in all the details of my escape. Telling the story very soon relieved me of my embarrassment as to my clothes. The horrible tales of Southern prison pens, however, was nothing new to General Sherman, for he related to me some of the awful things he had heard of Andersonville while his army was at Atlanta.

"At one time," said he, "I had great hopes of rescuing all of them at one quick blow. I gave General Stoneman a large body of cavalry, with directions to raid down about Macon. This raid was to go farther, and, by a quick, secret dash capture Andersonville and release every prisoner there. It was a chance to do the noblest deed of the war, but it all failed miserably. Stoneman had not fully obeyed orders, and, instead of releasing a whole army of suffering captives, he got captured himself, and, with him, a lot of my best cavalry."

It happened that I saw General Stoneman the very day he was brought to the prison. My narrative of how by desperately bold and violent cursing he denounced and defied his captors, and everything in Rebeldom, greatly amused Sherman and all at the table.

Stoneman's awful language and flashing eyes did indeed fairly intimidate the officer in charge. Evidently he thought he had captured a tiger. It was a wonder Stoneman was not killed.

The conversation about the prisoners continued. Twenty-five thousand of them were starving and dying in Andersonville. "It is one of the awful fates of war," said the general. "It can't be helped; they would have been better off had all been killed on the battlefield; and one almost wishes they had been." After a pause, he continued. "At times, I am almost satisfied it would be just as well to *kill all prisoners*." The remark, to me, a prisoner just escaped, seemed shocking. I am sure he noticed it, for he soon added: "They would be spared these atrocities. Besides, *the more awful you can make war the sooner it will be over*."

It would, after all, be a mercy.

"*War is hell, at the best,*" he went on, half in anger, and using an expression common to him.

For the moment I thought him heartless, but other remarks made to me, and to the staff, soon told us that whatever the cruelties imposed on him as a commander, they were executed with heart-pain and only as plain duty for the salvation of his own army. He even talked of how glad he would be to be out of the whole bloody business, once the Union were restored. But if the rebellion continued all his life, he would stay and fight it out.

When the dinner was over each looked about him to find some garment to give me. This one had an extra coat, that one a pair of trousers, and another one a hat. In short I was quickly attired in a rather respectable uniform.

This matter was just about ended when a beautiful woman was conducted to Sherman, to ask protection for her home, that was in his line of march. She was "true blue Union," despite her surroundings. In a moment the whole atmosphere about the tent was changed. The red-handed warrior, who a moment before was ready to kill even prisoners, suddenly became the most amiable, the most gallant and knightly looking man I ever saw. Beauty, that can draw a soldier with a single hair, had ensnared the great commander. He had become a gentle knight. The whole army if need be, would stand stock still to do her one little favour. I now recall how long after the war I noticed a hundred times this perfectly knightly gallantry of Sherman toward all women.

This one particular woman seemed a hundred times more beauti-ful, more fascinating, there in the green wood alone, with an army of a hundred thousand strangers about her, when, pointing her hand toward a great banner that swung in the wind between two tall pines, she smiled and cried:"General Sherman, *THAT IS MY FLAG TOO.*" There was a clapping of hands from all of us, and any one of us would have been glad to be sent as the protector of her home.

The great army was now marching, or rather swimming and wad-ing, in the direction of Fayetteville, N. C. There were heavy rains and the country, naturally swampy, was flooded everywhere. I soon learned from the staff where the army had already been. After the end of the march to the sea and the capture of Savannah, Sherman had started in with sixty thousand men, to treat South Carolina in the manner he had treated Georgia—march through it and desolate it. His proposed march northward from Savannah was regarded by the Southern gen-erals as an impossibility. The obstacles were so great as to make it a hundred times as difficult as his march from Atlanta to the sea. But he led a great army of picked veterans, accustomed to everything, whose flags had almost never known defeat. Their confidence in their general and in themselves was simply absolute. So far, in their march from Savannah they had hesitated at nothing.

It was midwinter, and yet that army had often waded in swamps with the cold water waist deep, carrying their clothes and their muskets on their heads. Half the roads they followed had to be corduroyed, or their horses would all have been lost in the bottomless mire and swamps. Often their artillery was for miles pulled along by the men themselves, and that in the face of the enemy, hidden behind every stream, and ready to ambush them at every roadside. Over all these infamous wagon roads, across all these bridgeless rivers and endless swamps, our army now dragged with it a train of sixty-nine cannon, twenty-five hundred six-mule wagons, and six hundred ambulances.

The tremendous obstacles they encountered before reaching Columbia they were again to encounter beyond. Not a bridge was left on any creek or river in the Carolinas. Roads were built of poles and logs through swamps ten miles wide. Sherman's army had few rations and no tents. The foragers brought in all the food they could pick up near the line of march. The little rubber blankets the soldiers carried were their sole protection from storm. They were almost shoeless. There were not a dozen full tents in the army. Officers used tent flies sometimes, but oftener simply rolled themselves up in their blankets, as their men did. At army headquarters we had but one large tent, used generally for dining under; so we usually slept in deserted cabins at the roadside.

I recall one fearfully stormy night when the general and his staff had all crept into a little church we found in the woods. The general would not accept the bit of carpet one of us had improvised into a bed for him on the pulpit platform. "No," he said, "keep that for some of you young fellows who are not well." He then stretched himself out on a wooden bench for the night. I think he never removed his uniform during the campaign. Day and night he was alert, and seemed never to be really asleep. We of the staff now had little to do save carrying orders occasionally to other commanders.

General Sherman did most of his own writing, and he wrote a rapid, beautiful hand. We had breakfast by the light of the campfire almost every morning, and were immediately in the saddle, floundering along through the mud, always near to, or quite at, the head of the army. At noon we always dismounted and ate a simple lunch at the roadside, sometimes washed down by a little whisky. Now and then some one of the army, recognizing the general riding past, would give a cheer that would be taken up by brigades and divisions a mile away. There seemed to be something peculiar about this Sherman cheer, for soldiers far off would cry out: "Listen to them cheering Billy Sherman."

On the 3rd of March we took Cheraw, and twenty-four cannon, also nearly four thousand barrels of gunpowder. That day General Logan, General Howard, General Kilpatrick, General Hazen, and many other notables came to headquarters. There was a jolly time of rejoicing.

Here General Logan, who could play the violin, entertained them by singing my song of "Sherman's March to the Sea," accompanying his voice with the instrument. A dozen famous generals joined in the chorus. After the singing, Logan insisted that I should also recite the poem. I did so, meeting with great applause from the very men who had been the leaders in the great "March." Alas! save one or two, they are now all dead.

Among the captures that day had been eight wagonloads of fine, old wine. It was now distributed among the different headquarters of the Union army, and as a result some of the said headquarters were pretty nearly drunk. One of our staff, at dinner the next day, attempted to explain his condition of the day before. "Never mind explaining," said General Sherman crustily, and without looking up, "but only see that the like of that does not happen again; that is all." That staff officer was a very sober man the rest of the campaign.

While we were lying there in Cheraw we heard an awful explosion; the very earth shook. I supposed it to be an earthquake until a messenger brought word that a lot of captured gunpowder had exploded and killed and wounded twenty soldiers.

As we were crossing on our pontoons over the Pedee River at Cheraw I noticed a singular way of punishing army thieves. An offender of this kind stood on the bridge, guarded by two sentinels. He was inside of a barrel that had the ends knocked out. On the barrel in big letters were the words: "I am a thief." The whole army corps passed close by him. An occasional man indulged in some joke at his expense, but the body of soldiers affected not to see him. The day we entered Cheraw General Sherman and his staff rode through the country alone for ten miles, going across from one column to another. It was a hazardous ride, as the whole country was full of guerrillas. But nothing of note happened to us.

On the 8th of March the headquarters staff was bivouacked in the woods near Laurel Hill. The army was absolutely cut off from everywhere. It had no base; it was weeks since Sherman had heard from the North or since the North had heard from him. Now he resolved to try to get a courier with a message through to Wilmington, at the seaside. An experienced spy by the name of Pike was selected to float down the Cape Fear River to ask the commander to try to send a tugboat up, to communicate with the army. I did not know then that the next one to run down Cape Fear River would be myself.

In four days we had taken Fayetteville and its wonderful arsenal, built years before by the American people, and where now half the war supplies of the Rebel army were made.

When the general and his staff first rode into Fayetteville headquarters were established in the arsenal. The general, wishing to look about the town for an hour or so, left me in charge. The other officers rode away with him. Very shortly a well-dressed, fine-looking old Southerner came to me and complained that his home was being disturbed by some of our soldiers. He was, he said, an old West Point friend of General Sherman's. While waiting the return of the commander, he regaled me with incidents of their early days together in the North and with his intimacies with one who would now doubtless be overwhelmed with joy at seeing him. He begged me to observe what would be his reception when the general should come. Impressed by his conversation, I at once sent a soldier or two to guard his home.

Shortly after General Sherman rode in through the arsenal portal and dismounted. The Southerner advanced with open arms, and for a moment there was a ray of pleasure illuminating Sherman's face. Then he went and leaned against a column, and, turning to the Southerner, said, "Yes, we were long together, weren't we?"

"Yes," answered the Southerner, delighted.

"You shared my friendship, shared my bread, even, didn't you?" continued Sherman.

"Indeed, indeed!" the Southerner replied, with increasing warmth.

The general gave the Southerner a long, steady, almost pathetic look, and answered, "You have betrayed it all; me, your friend, your country that educated you for its defence. You are here a traitor, and you ask me to be again your friend, to protect your property, to send you these brave men, some of whose comrades were murdered by your neighbours this very morning—fired on from hidden houses by you and yours as they entered the town. Turn your back to me forever. I will not punish you; only go your way. There is room in the world even for traitors." The Southerner turned ashy white and walked away from us in silence. Sherman sat down with the rest of us to our noonday lunch. We sat about the portal on stones, or barrels, or whatever happened to answer for seats. The general could scarcely eat. Never had I seen him under such emotion; the corners of his mouth twitched as he continued talking to us of this false friend. The hand that held the bread trembled and for a moment tears were in his eyes. For a little while we all sat in silence, and we realized as never before what treason to the republic really meant. The general spoke as if he, nor we, might ever live through it all.

Very soon General Howard rode in to complain anew of the outrages committed on our troops by men firing from windows as they passed along the streets. Two or three soldiers had been killed.

"Who did this outrage?" cried Sherman, in a loud and bitter voice.

"Texans, I think," answered General Howard.

"Then shoot some Texan prisoners in retaliation," said Sherman sternly.

"We have no Texans," replied Howard, not inclined, apparently, to carry out the serious, but just order.

"Then take other prisoners, take any prisoners," continued General Sherman. "I will not permit my soldiers to be murdered." He turned on his heel and walked away. Howard mounted and rode into the town. What happened, I do not know.

On Sunday morning General Sherman asked me to take a walk with him through the immense arsenal of Fayetteville before he should blow it up. We were gone an hour, and I was surprised at his great familiarity with all the machinery and works of the immense establishment. He talked constantly and explained many things to me. Never more than at that time was I impressed with the universal knowledge, the extraordinary genius, of the man. There seemed to be nothing there he did not understand.

On our way back to headquarters I heard him give the order to destroy everything, to burn the arsenal down, blow it up, to leave absolutely nothing, and he added the prayer that the American government might never again give North Carolina an arsenal and forts to betray. He was very angry now at those who had used the United States property in their desire to destroy the government itself. He had seen nothing in the war that seemed so treasonable, unless it was the base ingratitude of those who entered the service of the Rebellion after having been educated at West Point at the government's expense.

Pretty soon he said to me: "If I can get any kind of a boat up here, I am going to have you try to reach Wilmington with dispatches."

Almost at that minute a steam whistle sounded in the woods below us. "There it is," said the general joyfully. "Pike got through." Very soon someone came running to say a communication had come from the seashore; a little tug had run the Rebel gauntlet all the way from Wilmington.

We went in to lunch and the general announced to the staff his intention of sending me down the river, and off to General Grant with dispatches. This chance to get word of his movements and his successes to General Grant and the North was of vast importance, and it moved him greatly. He left his lunch half finished and commenced writing letters and reports to the commander-in-chief. That evening at twilight General Sherman walked with me down to the riverside where the little tug lay waiting. "When you reach the North," he said, putting his arm around me, "don't tell them we have been cutting any great swath in the Carolinas; simply tell them the plain facts; tell them that the army is not lost, but is well, and still marching." So careful was I as to his injunctions, that even the newspapers at Washington never knew how the great news from Sherman reached the North.

I did not know then, starting down the river with my message, that it was to be seven years before I was again to see the face of my beloved commander.

The Cape Fear River was flooded at this time, a mile wide, in places even more, and though its banks were lined with guerrillas there could not be great danger, if we could stay in the middle of the stream, unless our little boat should get wrecked in the darkness by floating trees or by running into shallow places. The lights were all put out. The pilot house and the sides of the boat were covered by bales of cotton, to protect us against the Rebel bullets. My dispatches to General Grant were carefully sewed up inside my shirt, and were weighted, so that I could hastily sink them in the river should we be captured.

A half dozen refugees from Columbia joined us. Among them was the Mrs. C——, whose property Devine and I had tried to save the night of the fire. It was a curious and dangerous voyage down that roaring, flooded river for a woman to be undertaking in the darkness, but this woman had now undertaken many dangers. Another of my companions on that strange voyage was Theodore Davis, a corresponding artist of *Harper's Weekly*. We kept the boat in the channel as far as we could guess it, and, for the rest, simply floated in the darkness. We went through undiscovered; not a shot fired at us. Before daylight, so swift had been the current, we were in Wilmington.

General Terry had just taken Wilmington and was in command of the city. Some of my dispatches were for him. He was still in bed, in one of the fine residences of the place, but instantly arose and urged me to jump into bed and get some rest while he should arrange to get me immediate transportation to Grant. I slept till nine, and when I came down to the drawing-room, now used as headquarters, General Terry asked if perhaps it were I who wrote the song about Sherman's March from Atlanta seaward. It had been sung at the theatre the night before, he said. I was much gratified to have him tell me that the whole army had taken it up. "Tens of thousands of men," he said, "were singing it." I knew, as already told, that an exchanged prisoner had brought the song through the Rebel lines in an artificial leg he wore, but it was an agreeable surprise to now learn of its sudden and tremendous success.

General Terry impressed me as the handsomest soldier I had seen in the army—McPherson, the commander of my own corp., only excepted. He was, too, a refined and perfect gentleman. Looking at him I thought of the cavaliers of romance. Here was real knighthood, born and bred in the soil of the republic. The laurels for his heroic capture of Fort Fisher were fresh on his brow.

Before noon an ocean steamer, the *Edward Everett*, was ordered to take me at once to Fortress Monroe. Two of my army friends went along. The captain, leaving on so short notice, had provided his ship with insufficient ballast, and to me, a landsman, the vessel's lurchings were very astonishing. I had never seen the ocean before, and it was not long till I wished I might never see it again. To add to my alarm, a fierce tempest sprang up as we passed around Cape Hatteras, and the danger was no longer imaginary, but very real. The few passengers on the boat might as well have been dead, so far as any self-help was to be thought of in case of disaster. Even the captain was very seasick, and, altogether, passengers and crew were badly scared. For many hours it was nothing but a fierce blow and a roll about on the mad waters.

All things come to an end; so did this storm, and at last we reached Fortress Monroe, where I was hurriedly transferred by some sailors in a yawl over to a boat that had already started up the James toward Richmond. Our captain had signalled that he had a dispatch bearer from the Carolinas. We had not gone far until we passed the top of a ship's mast sticking a few feet above the water. It was the mast of the *Cumberland*, that had gone down in her fight with the *Merrimac* with as brave a crew as ever manned a war boat.

The steamer I was now on was crowded with officers in bright uniforms, apparently returning to their regiments. I wondered if all the Eastern army had been home on a furlough. I could not help contrasting to myself this ship full of sleek, brightly uniformed officers with the rough-clad soldiers and officers of the army of Sherman. Sherman's foragers and veterans of the March to the Sea might have cut an awkward figure alongside these gay youths just from Washington.

In the afternoon the ship came to at City Point, and I climbed up the bank of the river bluff for perhaps a hundred feet, and was soon directed to the headquarters of the commander-in-chief of the United States armies.

When I reached the open door of Grant's famous little cabin a young officer asked me to come in, and was introducing me to the chief of staff, Rawlins, who stood there with some letters in his hands. That instant General Grant showed his face at the door in the back of the room. I knew who it was at once. He stepped forward to where General Rawlins was speaking with me, listened to the conversation a moment, and without any formal introduction, smiled, took me by the hand and led me into the back room of the cabin shutting the door behind us. He asked me to sit down, but I first proceeded to rip the dispatches out of my clothing, and with intense interest watched his features while he sat on a camp stool by the window, his legs crossed, and read Sherman's letter. I could see the glow of silent satisfaction as he glanced along the lines that told of his great lieutenant's successes in the South. He glanced at another letter I held in my hand. "It is for the President," I said. "He will be here yet to-night," he answered. "His boat must now be coming up the bay."

Then General Grant questioned me as to all I knew about Sherman's army, the character of the opposition he had met, the condition of his soldiers, their clothing, the roads, the weather. He also asked me how I had reached him with the dispatches, coming all the way from the interior of North Carolina. He seemed to have thought for a moment that I had come across Virginia on foot. He wanted to know of me again about the terrible treatment of prisoners in the South. What I told him only "confirmed," he said, what he had heard from a hundred sources.

Very shortly he heard the voice of General Ord in the outer room.

"Come in here, Ord," he said, holding the door open. "Come in and hear the news from Sherman. Look at that, listen to this," and again he went through Sherman's letter, reading parts of it aloud.

"Good! Good!" cried Ord, fairly dancing about the cabin, his spurs and sabre jingling. "I was really getting afraid."

"Not I, not I, not a bit," exclaimed Grant enthusiastically, as he rose to his feet. "*I knew my man. I knew General Sherman.*"

I was astonished now at the simple and perfectly frank manner with which General Grant talked to me about the situation of the army. I had ventured to ask if there was any outlook for the immediate fall of Richmond or a battle.

"Very great," he answered. "I am only afraid Lee may slip out before we can get a great blow at him. Any hour this may happen." Just then there was cannonading. I wondered if a fight were commencing somewhere in the line already. General Grant did not change a muscle in his face. "Send out and see what the firing is," he said to an officer quietly, and then as quietly continued talking, asking me to tell him all I knew of a recent escapade of Kilpatrick and his cavalry. It happened that I knew all about it. Only a couple of weeks before Kilpatrick and his headquarters had been surprised in bed at a bivouac on the flank of Sherman's army, and were surrounded and some were captured. By a heroic struggle the cavalry leader had escaped his captors, had instantly rallied his troops there in the dark woods and given the bold Rebels a little drubbing.

The next day I had been with Sherman at headquarters and listened to Kilpatrick's recital of his adventure. My own narration of the night's cavalry fight, reciting how the cavalrymen and his aids dashed about with nothing on but their shirts, made General Grant smile very audibly. "I had expected the whole thing to be about as you say," he exclaimed, in a grateful way, "but the Richmond newspapers which fell into my hands made a big thing of the so-called capture of Sherman's cavalry leader."

Once, as the general rose and stood directly in front of us, I was astonished to see how small he seemed. I had seen Grant before, but on horseback or in battle, and, somehow, I had always regarded him as a rather large, solidly built man. Today in the little back room of his cabin, talking with him, I saw how mistaken I had been. General Grant, as I now saw him, was, in fact, a little man. Several times he rose and walked about the room. He was not more than five feet seven or eight inches high, and he could not have weighed more than one hundred and forty or fifty pounds. He wore a simple fatigue uniform, and his coat thrown open gave him the appearance of being larger chested than he really was. His brown hair was neither short nor long, and he wore a full beard, well trimmed.

Had I not known to whom I was talking, or had I not seen the three stars on his shoulders, I would have supposed myself in the presence of some simple army captain. There was nothing whatever about him to announce the presence of genius or extraordinary ability of any kind. He was in no sense a striking-looking man. His manner and words to me were kind and earnest. There was an agreeable look about his mouth and eyes that made him seem very sincere. Indeed, if any one thing about him impressed me more than another, it was his apparent sincerity and earnestness. And he looked to me like a man of great common sense. Of vanity, pretence, or power there was not a single sign. He could not have looked very greatly different when he was hewing logs for his house at his father-in-law's farm ten years before, from what he looked just now, quietly directing a million soldiers in the greatest war of modern times.

Like General Sherman, he repeatedly expressed his interest concerning the terrible experiences I had undergone in Southern prisons.

"I suppose you will want to get home as quickly as possible, won't you?" he inquired, "or would you rather remain here awhile and look about the army?" A steamer was to leave for the North in an hour. Privately, I was fearing a sudden break-down of my health, and longed for a home that I had visited but eight days during four long years of war. Then I thought of my letter to Mr. Lincoln. The general seemed to anticipate my thought. "Leave the President's letter with me," he said, "if you choose, and I will give it to him, or stay over and give it to him yourself."

There was no man living I was so anxious to see as Abraham Lincoln. And this was my opportunity. But something like a premonition said, "Go home." When I expressed my feeling General Grant stepped to the door of the office room and directed General Rawlins to see that I be provided with leave of absence and transportation. That little order, signed by Rawlins, I still possess.

With an earnest handshake and goodbye General Grant thanked me for bringing him the dispatches. I was not to see him again for many years.[1]

---

1. At the town of Lucerne in Switzerland there is in front of the Schweizerhof a quay lined with castanien trees. It overlooks the beautiful (continued next page)

lake. Long years after the war General Grant sat there on a bench one quiet summer night and talked to me of the time I brought the news to him from Sherman in the Carolinas. In a few weeks from that night by the lakeside I had the honour of entertaining my old commander at my own home, in the city of Zurich, where I was now representing the government as one of his appointees. The order naming me to go to Zurich had, on a certain time, been written by his own hand.

This night at Zurich proved to be almost the last time I was ever to see the great commander. His presence and words that evening are among the treasured memories of my life.

CHAPTER 15

The Last Man of the Regiment

Leaving General Grant's headquarters at City Point was for me a final goodbye to the army. The little steamer *Martin* carried me down the James River, up the Chesapeake Bay, and the Potomac, toward the North. I recall now the strange sensations I had in passing Washington's tomb at Mount Vernon. The green slopes and the oak wood in front of the old mansion were in full view. I could even see the front columns of the house, and someone on the steamer's deck pointed out to me the spot where stood the simple brick mausoleum where with folded arms slept the Father of his Country. I could not help reflecting that at that moment not a hundred miles away stood nearly all George Washington's State's descendants, with arms in their hands, striving to destroy the government that he had founded.

How I enjoyed that ship ride! Here there was no sandy prison pen with poor, starving, dying comrades lying around; no futile efforts at escape; no taunts and jeers that the American flag had gone down in disgrace; now all was free and beautiful, and *mine*. The hated rag of the Confederacy that had floated over my head and threatened me every day with death for fifteen long months was gone forever. At the mast of our little vessel waved the Stars and Stripes, conscious, it seemed, to me, of the free air I was breathing. That was a happy day for me.

Sometime in the following night the wheels of the boat stopped revolving—there was silence; and when I woke at daylight there was the land. The ship was fast in the slip at the wharf, and there, too, was the capital of the republic. I went ashore by myself and wandered into the city, my mind crowded every moment with the thoughts of what had taken place here in the last four years. Soldiers I saw everywhere, with arms and without arms. Negroes, now freedmen, by the ten thousand fairly darkened the population. With some friends I found a boarding place on the avenue above the National Hotel. If I wanted to see great men, notorious men, men making history, all kinds of men, I had only to step into the corridors of the National.

I had little or no ready money, nor could I get any until the government settled my accounts. I waited in Washington for a week. General Sherman had given me papers that would insure my promotion in the regular army. I presented them; they were all-sufficient; I needed only to say the word. But I was sick and tired of war, and would not have exchanged a glimpse of my Western home for the commission of a brigadier.

But while I stayed in Washington what sights I saw! Our capital is now possibly the finest in the world. Then it was the most hateful; the most hateful in every way. Militarism, treason, political scoundrelism, and every other bad ism reigned in every hotel, on every street corner, in Congress, out of Congress—everywhere; reigned right at the elbows of loyalty and patriotism such as the world never saw. Society was one grand conglomeration of everything good and bad.

Washington City itself was a spectacle. It had no streets, save one or two—simply dirty unpaved roads. The dirty street cars, pulled by worn-out horses, were crowded inside and outside by a mass of struggling politicians, soldiers, gamblers, adventurers, and women. The city was also full of hospitals; everywhere there were lazarettos and graveyards. It looked as if half the Union army had dragged itself into the capital to die. The great Capital building was uncompleted; its dome stood there covered with scaffoldings and windlasses. The *plaza* at the east end of the structure looked like a vast stone quarry. The Washington Monument had only gotten itself safe above high-water mark; and what there was of it was in danger of falling down. It stood in the middle of the flats, the mud and the malaria—the graveyard, in short, that formed the unsavoury prospect from the White House windows.

Aside from the unfinished government buildings there was not a pretence of architecture in all Washington. There was nothing beautiful there. The very atmosphere seemed sickly; fever, malaria, were everywhere. It was the one city in all creation to get out of as soon as possible.

Once I tried to get a glimpse of the President. I failed. The White House gates were held by sentries. "Why do you want to see that old Ape?" said a man to me one day. I was shocked, and would like to have killed him. But he was not alone in his vileness. Thousands in Washington affected to despise Lincoln. I wondered then that it was

110

regarded safe for him to appear in public. One day a carriage rolled rapidly up the avenue in front of the National. I heard some men cry, "Look, the President!" I glanced quickly. A tall, dark man, wearing a silk hat sat in the carriage; at his side a lady.

In a moment they were out of sight. There was not a cheer, not a hat touched, not a hand waved, and yet *that was Abraham Lincoln passing*, soon to be the greatest man in history. A little wrangle and almost a fist-fight between some bystanders on the pavement followed; one party denouncing the President for freeing the "damned niggers"; another thanking God for the President's noble deed. Such scenes were going on everywhere all over the capital, pro and con. Approval and hatred. The best praised, the worst abused mortal in America was just entering on his second term at the White House. I never even had a glimpse of the kindly face again.

At last my accounts were ready. "But your regiment," said the Assistant War Secretary, "does not exist. What was left of them were all put into a cavalry troop long ago. *You are the last man of the regiment.*" Across the face of my paper he wrote, "*Discharged as a supernumerary officer.*" That paper lies before me while I write. I was paid off in shining greenbacks for all the time I had been in prison.

As to the eighty comrades who had been captured with me that 25th of November in the assault on Missionary Ridge, all but sixteen were dead. Nine of my old Company B of the Fifth Regiment were taken prisoners, and only one of them had survived the horrors of Andersonville. Poor Cartwright died not long after, and I alone of the little band was left to tell the story.

www.ingramcontent.com/pod-product-compliance
Lightning Source LLC
Chambersburg PA
CBHW031858090426
42741CB00005B/553